Nearest Neighbor Search

A Database Perspective

SERIES IN COMPUTER SCIENCE

Series Editor: **Rami G. Melhem**
University of Pittsburgh
Pittsburgh, Pennsylvania

DYNAMIC RECONFIGURATION
Architectures and Algorithms
Ramachandran Vaidyanathan and Jerry L. Trahan

ENGINEERING ELECTRONIC NEGOTIATIONS
A Guide to Electronic Negotiation Technologies for the Design and Implementation of Next-Generation Electronic Markets—Future Silkroads of eCommerce
Michael Ströbel

HIERARCHICAL SCHEDULING IN PARALLEL AND CLUSTER SYSTEMS
Sivarama Dandamudi

MOBILE IP
Present State and Future
Abdul Sakib Mondal

NEAREST NEIGHBOR SEARCH
A Database Perspective
Apostolos N. Papadopoulos and Yannis Manolopoulos

OBJECT-ORIENTED DISCRETE-EVENT SIMULATION WITH JAVA
A Practical Introduction
José M. Garrido

A PARALLEL ALGORITHM SYNTHESIS PROCEDURE FOR HIGH-PERFORMANCE COMPUTER ARCHITECTURES
Ian N. Dunn and Gerard G. L. Meyer

PERFORMANCE MODELING OF OPERATING SYSTEMS USING OBJECT-ORIENTED SIMULATION
A Practical Introduction
José M. Garrido

POWER AWARE COMPUTING
Edited by Robert Graybill and Rami Melhem

THE STRUCTURAL THEORY OF PROBABILITY
New Ideas from Computer Science on the Ancient Problem of Probability Interpretation
Paolo Rocchi

Nearest Neighbor Search

A Database Perspective

Apostolos N. Papadopoulos and Yannis Manolopoulos
Department of Informatics
Aristotle University
Thessaloniki, Greece

ISBN 0-387-22963-9

©2005 Springer Science+Business Media, Inc.
All rights reserved. This work may not be translated or copied in whole or in part without the written permission of the publisher (Springer Science+Business Media, Inc., 233 Spring Street, New York, NY 10013, USA), except for brief excerpts in connection with reviews or scholarly analysis. Use in connection with any form of information storage and retrieval, electronic adaptation, computer software, or by similar or dissimilar methodology now known or hereafter developed is forbidden.
The use in this publication of trade names, trademarks, service marks and similar terms, even if they are not identified as such, is not to be taken as an expression of opinion as to whether or not they are subject to proprietary rights.

Printed in the United States of America.   (BS/DH)

9 8 7 6 5 4 3 2 1

springeronline.com

Contents

List of Figures ix
List of Tables xiii
Preface xvii
Acknowledgments xxi

Part I Fundamental Issues

1. SPATIAL DATABASE CONCEPTS 3
   1   Introduction 3
   2   Spatial Query Processing 4
   3   Access Methods 6
   4   Handling High-Dimensional Data 8
   5   Spatial Data Support in Commercial Systems 9
   6   Summary 10
   7   Further Reading 11

2. THE R-TREE AND VARIATIONS 13
   1   Introduction 13
   2   The Original R-tree 13
   3   Dynamic R-tree Variants 15
       3.1   The R^+-tree 15
       3.2   The R*-tree 16
       3.3   The Hilbert R-tree 16
   4   Static R-tree Variants 17
       4.1   The Packed R-tree 18
       4.2   The Hilbert Packed R-tree 18

		4.3	The STR Packed R-tree	18
	5	Performance Issues		18
	6	R-trees in Emerging Applications		19
	7	Summary		20
	8	Further Reading		20

Part II Nearest Neighbor Search in Spatial and Spatiotemporal Databases

3.	NEAREST NEIGHBOR QUERIES			25
	1	Introduction		25
	2	The Nearest Neighbor Problem		25
	3	Applications		27
	4	Nearest Neighbor Queries in R-trees		28
	5	Nearest Neighbor Queries in Multimedia Applications		31
	6	Summary		34
	7	Further Reading		34
4.	ANALYSIS OF NEAREST NEIGHBOR QUERIES			37
	1	Introduction		37
	2	Analytical Considerations		38
		2.1	Preliminaries	38
		2.2	Estimation of d_{nn} and d_m	40
		2.3	Performance Estimation	42
	3	Performance Evaluation		44
		3.1	Preliminaries	44
		3.2	Experimental Results	45
	4	Summary		45
	5	Further Reading		47
5.	NEAREST NEIGHBOR QUERIES IN MOVING OBJECTS			49
	1	Introduction		49
	2	Organizing Moving Objects		50
	3	Nearest Neighbor Queries		52
		3.1	The NNS Algorithm	56
		3.1.1	Algorithm NNS-a	57
		3.1.2	Algorithm NNS-b	61
		3.2	Query Processing with TPR-trees	62

	4	Performance Evaluation	66
		4.1 Preliminaries	66
		4.2 Experimental Results	68
	5	Summary	71
	6	Further Reading	72

Part III Nearest Neighbor Search with Multiple Resources

6. PARALLEL AND DISTRIBUTED DATABASES — 75
   1. Introduction — 75
   2. Multidisk Systems — 76
   3. Multiprocessor Systems — 80
   4. Distributed Systems — 83
   5. Summary — 84
   6. Further Reading — 85

7. MULTIDISK QUERY PROCESSING — 87
   1. Introduction — 87
   2. Algorithms — 88
      - 2.1 The Branch-and-Bound Algorithm — 88
      - 2.2 Full-Parallel Similarity Search — 88
      - 2.3 Candidate Reduction Similarity Search — 91
      - 2.4 Optimal Similarity Search — 97
   3. Performance Evaluation — 98
      - 3.1 Preliminaries — 98
      - 3.2 Experimental Results — 102
      - 3.3 Interpretation of Results — 105
   4. Summary — 107
   5. Further Reading — 108

8. MULTIPROCESSOR QUERY PROCESSING — 109
   1. Introduction — 109
   2. Performance Estimation — 110
   3. Parallel Algorithms — 111
      - 3.1 Adapting BB-NNF in Declustered R-trees — 111
      - 3.2 The Parallel Nearest Neighbor Finding (**P-NNF**) Method — 113
      - 3.3 When Statistics are not Available — 116

		3.4	Correctness of P-NNF Algorithms	117
	4	Performance Evaluation		117
		4.1	Preliminaries	117
		4.2	The Cost Model	118
		4.3	Experimental Results	120
		4.4	Interpretation of Results	122
	5	Summary		124
	6	Further Reading		125
9.	DISTRIBUTED QUERY PROCESSING			127
	1	Introduction		127
	2	Query Evaluation Strategies		129
		2.1	Algorithms	129
		2.2	Theoretical Study	130
		2.3	Analytical Comparison	139
	3	The Impact of Derived Data		142
	4	Performance Evaluation		146
		4.1	Preliminaries	146
		4.2	Cost Model Evaluation	146
		4.3	Experimental Results	147
	5	Discussion		150
	6	Summary		151
	7	Further Reading		151
Epilogue				153
References				157

List of Figures

1.1	Examples of spatial datasets.	4
1.2	Examples of range and NN queries in 2-d space.	5
1.3	Examples of spatial join queries.	6
1.4	A set of polygons and their corresponding MBRs.	7
1.5	Filter-refinement query processing.	8
1.6	Intersection and containment queries.	8
1.7	Mapping time series to multidimensional vectors.	9
2.1	An R-tree example.	14
2.2	An R^+-tree example.	16
2.3	Examples of space-filling curves in 2-d space.	17
2.4	MBRs of leaf nodes for R-tree, R*-tree and STR packed R-tree.	19
3.1	Examples of 2-NN and 4-NN queries using the L_2 norm.	26
3.2	Answering a 3-NN query by using repetitive range queries.	27
3.3	MINDIST and MINMAXDIST between a point P and two rectangles R_1 and R_2.	30
3.4	NN search algorithm for R-trees.	31
4.1	Two equivalent query execution plans.	37
4.2	(a): example of Proposition 4.1, (b): example of Proposition 4.2.	40
4.3	When the query point P coincides with a vertex of the MBR, then the maximum difference (σ) between $MINDIST$ and $MINMAXDIST$ is obtained.	42
4.4	Example of an enlarged data page.	43
4.5	Datasets used in the experiments.	44

5.1	Generation of a moving bounding rectangle.	51
5.2	A NN query example in a moving dataset.	52
5.3	Visualization of the distance between a moving object and a moving query.	55
5.4	Relative distance of objects with respect to a moving query.	55
5.5	Nearest neighbors of the moving query for $k = 2$ (top) and $k = 3$ (bottom).	56
5.6	The NNS-a algorithm.	59
5.7	The four different cases that show the relation of a new object to the current nearest neighbors.	62
5.8	The NNS-b algorithm.	63
5.9	The modify-CNN-list procedure.	64
5.10	Pruning techniques.	65
5.11	The NNS-CON algorithm.	66
5.12	Results for different values of the number of nearest neighbors.	69
5.13	CPU cost over I/O cost.	69
5.14	Results for different buffer capacities.	70
5.15	Results for different values of the travel time.	71
5.16	Results for different space dimensions.	71
5.17	Results for different database size.	72
6.1	Parallel and distributed database systems.	75
6.2	Example of disk array architecture.	77
6.3	Independent R-trees.	78
6.4	R-tree with super-nodes.	78
6.5	MX R-tree example.	79
6.6	Parallel architectures.	81
6.7	R-tree example.	82
6.8	Declustering an R-tree over three sites.	82
6.9	Horizontal and vertical fragmentation.	83
6.10	Distributed database architecture.	84
7.1	$MINDIST$, $MINMAXDIST$ and $MAXDIST$ between a point P and two rectangles R_1 and R_2.	90
7.2	Illustration of pruning and candidate selection.	91
7.3	Example of an R*-tree with 13 nodes and 3 entries per node.	93
7.4	Illustration of the first three stages of the **CRSS** algorithm. Different candidate runs are separated by guards, indicated by shaded boxes.	93

List of Figures

7.5	The most important code fragments of the **CRSS** algorithm.	95
7.6	Datasets used in performance evaluation.	99
7.7	The simulation model for the system under consideration.	100
7.8	Number of visited nodes vs. query size for 2-d data sets.	103
7.9	Number of visited nodes (normalized to **WOPTSS**) vs. query size for synthetic data in 10-d space.	103
7.10	Response time (secs) vs. query arrival rate (λ).	104
7.11	Response time (normalized to WOPTSS) vs. number of disks (λ=5 queries/sec, dimensions=5).	104
7.12	Response time (normalized to **WOPTSS**) vs. number of nearest neighbors (Left: λ=1 queries/sec, Right: λ=20 queries/sec).	104
7.13	**BBSS** will visit all nodes associated with the branch of R_1, leading to unnecessary accesses.	106
8.1	Declustering an R-tree over three sites.	109
8.2	Measured and Estimated number of leaf accesses vs. the number k of nearest neighbors.	112
8.3	Basic difference between **BB-NNF** and **P-NNF** methods.	114
8.4	$MINDIST, MINMAXDIST$ and $MAXDIST$ between a point P and two rectangles R_1 and R_2.	114
8.5	The IEEE 802.3 (CSMA/CD bus) frame layout.	118
8.6	Graphical representation of datasets used for experimentation.	119
8.7	Calculation of the Response Time of a query.	120
8.8	Response time (in msecs) vs. k (secondary sites=10, $NS_{eff} = 10Mbit/sec$).	121
8.9	Number of transmitted frames, time to process the upper R-tree levels and number of transmitted objects, vs. k (secondary sites=10, $NS_{eff} = 10Mbit/sec$).	122
8.10	Response time (in msecs) vs. number of secondary servers.	123
9.1	The abstract system architecture.	127
9.2	Performance of methods for scenario A (logarithmic scales).	140
9.3	Performance of methods for scenario B (logarithmic scales).	141
9.4	(a) Use of two MBBs for discrimination, (b) The nearest neighbor of P is not in MBB1, (c) A query point P enclosed by many MBBs.	143
9.5	Cost model evaluation (logarithmic scales).	147
9.6	Measured response time for scenario A (logarithmic scales).	148
9.7	Measured response time for scenario B (logarithmic scales).	150

List of Tables

3.1	Distances between a query object and some data objects.	33
4.1	Basic notations used throughout the analysis.	39
4.2	Number of leaf accesses vs. data population. Data=Uniform, Fanout=50.	46
4.3	Number of leaf accesses vs. fanout. Data=Uniform, Population=50,000.	46
4.4	Number of leaf accesses vs. fanout. Data=MG points, Population $\approx$ 9,000.	46
5.1	NN queries for different query and data characteristics.	54
5.2	Parameters and corresponding values.	67
5.3	Experiments conducted.	68
7.1	Description of query processing parameters.	101
7.2	Description of disk characteristics (model HP-C220A) [108].	101
7.3	Scalability with respect to population growth: Response time (secs) vs. population and number of disks. (set: gaussian, dimensions: 5, NNs: 20, λ=5 queries/sec).	105
7.4	Scalability with respect to query size growth: Response time (secs) vs. number of nearest neighbors and number of disks. (set: gaussian, dimensions: 5, population: 80,000, λ=5 queries/sec).	105
7.5	Qualitative comparison of all algorithms (a $\sqrt{}$ means good performance).	107
8.1	Description of datasets.	118
8.2	Response Time vs. network speed (Secondary sites=10, NN requested = 10, 100 and 200).	124
9.1	Symbols, definitions and corresponding values.	130

About the Authors

Apostolos N. Papadopoulos was born in Eleftheroupolis, Greece in 1971. He received his 5-year Diploma degree in Computer Engineering and Informatics from the University of Patras and his Ph.D. degree from Aristotle University of Thessaloniki in 1994 and 2000 respectively. He has published several research papers in journals and proceedings of international conferences. From March 1998 to August 1998 he was a visitor researcher at INRIA research center in Rocquencourt, France, to perform research in benchmarking issues for spatial databases. Currently, he is a Lecturer in the Department of Informatics of Aristotle University of Thessaloniki. He is a member of the Greek Computer Society and the Technical Chamber of Greece. His research interests include spatial and spatiotemporal databases, data stream processing, parallel and distributed databases, data mining, physical database design.

Yannis Manolopoulos was born in Thessaloniki, Greece in 1957. He received his 5-year Diploma degree in Electrical Engineering and his Ph.D. degree in Computer Engineering from Aristotle University of Thessaloniki in 1981 and 1986 respectively. Currently he is Professor at the Department of Informatics of the same university. He has been with the Department of Computer Science of the University of Toronto, the Department of Computer Science of the University of Maryland at College Park and the Department of Computer Science of the University of Cyprus. He has (co-)authored over 140 papers in refereed scientific journals and conference proceedings. He has also (co-)authored several textbooks in Greek and two monographs on "Advanced Database Indexing" and "Advanced Signature Indexing for Multimedia and Web Applications" by Kluwer. He served as PC (co-)chair of the 8th National Computer Conference (2001), the 6th ADBIS Conference (2002), the 5th WDAS Workshop (2003), the 8th SSTD Symposium (2003), the 1st Balkan Conference in Informatics (2003), and the 16th SSDBM Conference (2004). He is member of the Editorial Board of The Computer Journal and the International Journal of Data Warehousing and Mining. Also, he is Vice-chair of the Greek Computer Society and Chair of the Greek Section of ACM SIGKDD. His research interests include databases, data mining, data/file structures and algorithms, and performance evaluation of storage subsystems.

Preface

Modern applications are both data and computationally intensive and require the storage and manipulation of voluminous traditional (alphanumeric) and non-traditional data sets, such as images, text, geometric objects, time-series, audio, video. Examples of such emerging application domains are: geographical information systems (GIS), multimedia information systems, CAD/CAM, time-series analysis, medical information systems, on-line analytical processing (OLAP), data mining. These applications pose diverse requirements with respect to the information and the operations that need to be supported, and therefore from the database perspective, new techniques and tools need to be developed towards increased processing efficiency.

Spatial database management systems aims at supporting queries that involve the space characteristics of the underlying data. For example, a spatial database may contain polygons that represent building footprints from a satellite image or the representation of lakes, rivers and other natural objects. It is important to be able to query the database by using predicates that are related to the spatial and geometric object characteristics. Examples of such queries are:

- the range query: given a rectangle R, determine objects in the database that intersect R,

- the nearest neighbor query: given an object O, determine the k objects from the database that are closer to O,

- the spatial join query: given two sets of objects, determine the pairs that satisfy a spatial predicate (e.g., intersection, containment),

- the closest-pair query: given two sets of objects, determine the k pairs that have the k smallest distances amongst all possible pairs.

A spatial database system is enhanced by special tools to handle such queries. These tools include new data types, sophisticated data structures and algorithms for efficient query processing that differ from their counterparts in a conservative alphanumeric database. The contribution of the research community over the past twenty years includes a plethora of research works towards this goal.

Apart from exploiting novel techniques for efficient spatial query processing, another direction is to use multiple resources (processors and/or disks) towards more efficient processing. If several processors are used to solve a problem, the total processing time is likely to be reduced, due to the parallel execution of several independent operations. The purpose of this research monograph is to study efficient processing techniques for nearest neighbor search, by assuming a database point of view.

Intended Audience

This book can be used by students, researchers and professionals who are interested in nearest neighbor search and related issues. More specifically, the book will be a valuable companion for postgraduate students who are studying spatial database issues, and for instructors who can use the book as a reference for specialized topics in nearest neighbor query processing techniques. Researchers in several related areas will find this book useful, since it covers many important research directions.

Prerequisites

Each book chapter is self-contained to help the reader focus on the corresponding issue. Moreover, the partitioning of the chapters in parts will be very convenient in focusing in different research issues, according to the reader's needs. However, at least a basic knowledge in indexing, query processing and optimization in traditional database systems, will be very helpful in understanding more easily the issues covered by each chapter.

Book Organization

The content of this monograph is based on research performed by the authors in the Data Engineering Lab of the Department of Informatics of Aristotle University during the last years. The material is organized in three parts, composed of nine chapters in total, covering different issues related to nearest neighbor search.

In **Part I** we cover fundamental issues regarding spatial databases. This part is composed of three chapters. **Chapter 1** performs a gentle introduction to spatial database concepts, by discussing issues related to query processing, indexing and handling multidimensional datasets. In **Chapter 2** we focus on the R-tree family of spatial access methods, and discuss issues related to indexing spatial objects. Several important R-tree variations are also briefly presented.

Part II is composed of three chapters. **Chapter 3** discusses in detail nearest neighbor query processing in R-trees, applications of nearest neighbor search and some important issues regarding nearest neighbor search in multimedia database systems. In **Chapter 4** we study the issue of cost estimation in nearest neighbor queries using fractal concepts. Finally, **Chapter 5** studies nearest neighbor queries in spatiotemporal databases, and more specifically in moving objects databases. Querying moving objects poses new challenges since the answer to a query change over time, due to the continuous object movement.

Part III covers parallel and distributed processing of nearest neighbor queries. **Chapter 6** gives the appropriate background in parallel and distributed databases, and discusses several important issues. **Chapter 7** studies the problem of nearest neighbor query processing in a single-processor multidisk system. In such a system the dataset is declustered among all disks and therefore several disk access operations can be performed in parallel, reducing the query response time. Algorithms are presented and experimental results are given demonstrating the performance efficiency. **Chapter 8** studies nearest neighbor query processing in a system composed of many disks and many processors. The dataset and the corresponding access method are declustered among a number of computers. The challenge is to provide efficient processing techniques to answer the nearest neighbor query by exploiting parallelism. **Chapter 9** studies the problem in a similar environment, by allowing each computer to manage its own local database independently from the others.

In the **Epilogue** we give a brief summary of the book and raise some important issues for further research in the area.

APOSTOLOS N. PAPADOPOULOS

YANNIS MANOLOPOULOS

To our families.

Acknowledgments

The material of this monograph is based on research performed in the Data Engineering Lab of the Department of Informatics of the Aristotle University, during the last years. We are very grateful to all who supported us during the preparation of this monograph. Especially, we would like to thank our co-authors and colleagues Antonio Corral, Yannis Karidis, Dimitris Katsaros, Maria Kontaki, Alexandros Nanopoulos, Katerina Raptopoulou, Antonis Sidiropoulos, Yannis Theodoridis Theodoros Tzouramanis, Michael Vassilakopoulos and Dimitris Halvatzis for their helpful comments and suggestions. Moreover, we would like to thank Ana Bozicevic from Kluwer Academic Publishers, for her patience and encouragement towards the successful completion of this project.

I

FUNDAMENTAL ISSUES

Chapter 1

SPATIAL DATABASE CONCEPTS

1. Introduction

Modern applications are both data and computationally intensive and require the storage and manipulation of voluminous traditional (alphanumeric) and non-traditional data sets, such as images, text, geometric objects, time series, audio, video. Examples of such emerging application domains are: geographical information systems (GIS), multimedia information systems, time-series analysis, medical information systems, on-line analytical processing (OLAP) and data mining. These applications impose diverse requirements with respect to the information and the operations that need to be supported. Therefore from the database perspective, new techniques and tools need to be developed towards increased processing efficiency.

The exploitation of a DBMS towards efficient support of such applications is being considered mandatory to provide fast access and high data availability. However, since traditional DBMSs can not easily support such applications, new or modified components are needed. Faster storage managers should be developed; the query processor and the query optimizer must take into consideration the new data types; the transaction processor must be enhanced with special features to cope with the load posed by users, towards response time reduction and throughput increase.

The main goal of a *spatial database system* is the effective and efficient handling of *spatial data types* in two, three or higher dimensional spaces, and the ability to answer queries taking into consideration the spatial data properties. Examples of spatial data types are:

- *point*: characterized by a pair of (x,y) values,

- *line segment*: characterized by a pair of points,

- *rectangle*: characterized by its lower-left and upper-right corners,

- *polygon*: comprised by a set of points, defining its corners.

Figure 1.1 represents examples of spatial datasets. In Figure 1.1(a) the European countries are represented as polygons, whereas in Figure 1.1(b) a GIS map is shown which contains information about a specific geographic area of Northern Greece.

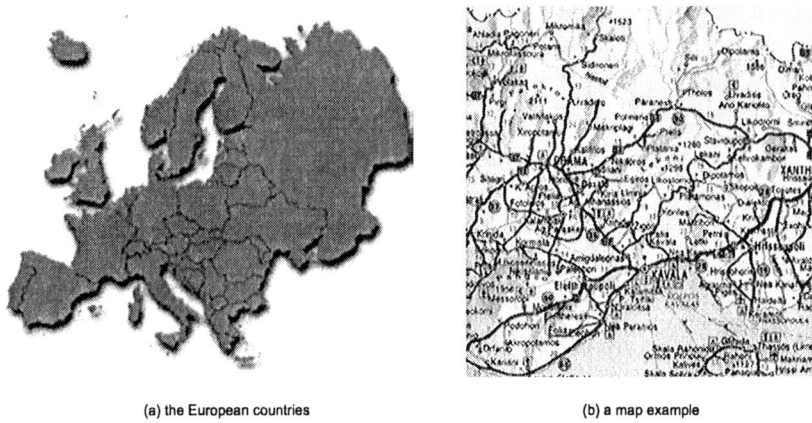

(a) the European countries (b) a map example

Figure 1.1. Examples of spatial datasets.

2. Spatial Query Processing

In traditional database systems user queries are usually expressed by SQL statements containing conditions among the attributes of the relations (database tables). A spatial database system must be equipped with additional functionality to answer queries containing conditions among the *spatial attributes* of the database objects, such as location, extend and geometry. The most common *spatial query types* are:

- *topological queries* (e.g., find all objects that overlap or cover a given object),

- *directional queries* (e.g., find all objects that lie north of a given object),

- *distance queries* (e.g., find all objects that lie in less than a given distance from a given object).

The aforementioned spatial operations comprise basic primitives for developing more complex ones in applications that are based on management of spatial data, such as GIS, cartography and many others. Let us examine three queries

Spatial Database Concepts 5

that are widely used in spatial applications and have been studied thoroughly in the literature:

- *range query*: is the most common topological query. A query area R is given and all objects that intersect or are contained in R are requested.

- *nearest neighbor (NN) query*: is the most common distance query. Given a query point P and a positive integer k, the query returns the k objects that are closer to P, based on a distance metric (e.g., Euclidean distance).

- *spatial join query*: is used to determine pairs of spatial objects that satisfy a particular property. Given two spatial datasets D_A and D_B and a predicate θ, the output of the spatial join query is a set of pairs O_a, O_b such that $O_a \in D_A$, $O_b \in D_B$ and $\theta(O_a, O_b)$ is true.

- *closest-pair query*: is a combination of spatial join and nearest neighbor queries. Given two spatial datasets D_A and D_B, the output of a k closest-pairs query is composed of k pairs O_a, O_b such that $O_a \in D_A$, $O_b \in D_B$. These k pair-wise distances are the smallest amongst all possible object pairs.

Figure 1.2 presents examples of range and NN queries for a database consisting of points in 2-d space. In Figure 1.2(a) the answer to the range query is comprised by the three data points that are enclosed by R. In Figure 1.2(b) the answer to the NN query is composed of the five data points that are closer to P.

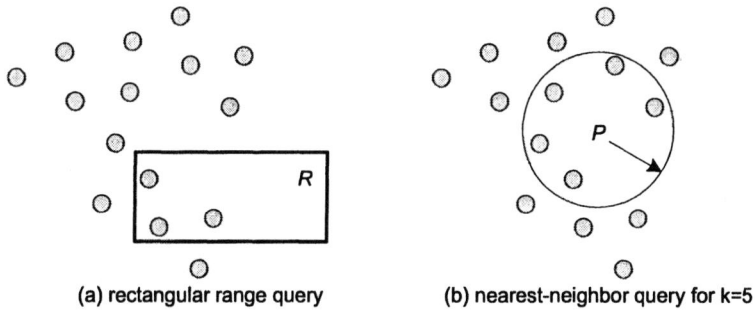

(a) rectangular range query   (b) nearest-neighbor query for k=5

Figure 1.2. Examples of range and NN queries in 2-d space.

Figure 1.3 gives two examples of spatial join queries. In Figure 1.3(a) the query asks for all intersecting pairs of the two datasets (intersection spatial join), whereas in Figure 1.3(b) the query asks for all pairs O_a, O_b such that O_b is totally enclosed by O_a (containment spatial join).

A spatial DBMS must efficiently support spatial queries. Towards this goal, the system must be able to select an efficient *query execution plan* (QEP) for

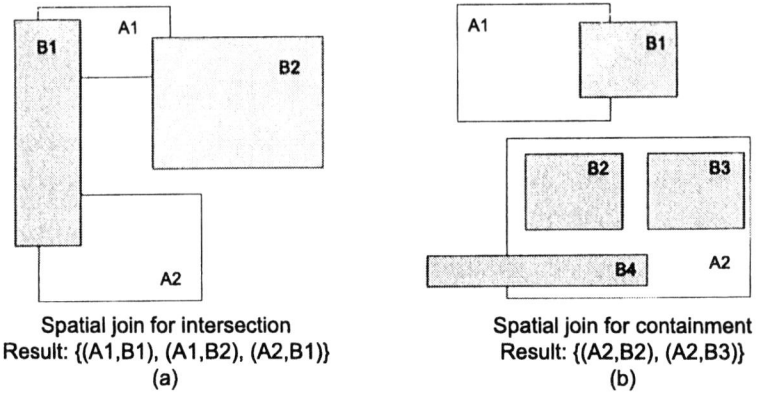

Figure 1.3. Examples of spatial join queries.

a complex spatial query. Determining the best execution plan for a spatial query requires tools for measuring (more precisely, estimating) the number of (spatial) data items that are retrieved by a query as well as its cost, in terms of I/O and CPU effort. As in traditional query optimization, such tools include cost-based optimization models, exploiting analytical formulae for selectivity (the hit percentage) and cost of a query, as well as histogram-based techniques.

In this book we focus on methods and techniques for the processing of NN queries. As we show later, NN queries play an important role not only in spatial database systems but in multimedia database systems as well, because they allow the retrieval of similar objects according to a distance metric.

3. Access Methods

The processing of spatial queries presents significant requirements, due to the large volumes of spatial data and the complexity of both objects and queries [85]. Efficient processing of spatial queries capitalize on the proximity of the objects to focus the searching on objects that satisfy the queries and eliminate the irrelevant ones. The target is to avoid the *sequential scanning* of the database which is an extremely costly operation.

In traditional database systems, access methods like B-trees and hashing offer considerable improvements in query response time in comparison to the sequential database scanning. Similarly, *spatial access methods* (SAMs) provide an efficient way of organizing the data and processing spatial queries. In several textbooks and research reports there is a differentiation between *point access methods* (PAMs), used to manipulate points, and *spatial access methods* (SAMs) used to manipulate arbitrary spatial objects. In this book we use the term SAM for both. Several spatial access methods have been proposed in the

Spatial Database Concepts

literature, with different characteristics and performance. Most of the proposed techniques are based on hierarchical (tree-like) structures and offer efficient processing to specific types of queries.

Most of the spatial access methods organize the underlying data based on *object approximation*. Therefore, complex spatial objects are approximated by simpler ones to support efficient indexing. The most common spatial approximation is the *minimum bounding rectangle* (MBR for short), which is the minimum rectangle that encloses the detailed object geometry. Figure 1.4 presents a set of polygons and their corresponding MBRs.

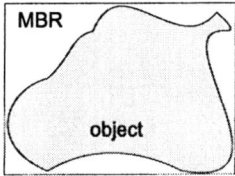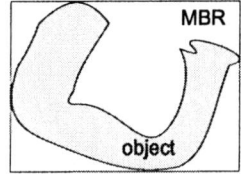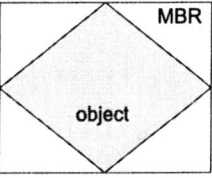

Figure 1.4. A set of polygons and their corresponding MBRs.

The majority of the access methods are used in conjunction with the *filter-refinement* processing paradigm. More specifically, to process a query a two-step procedure is followed, comprised by the following phases:

1 *filter phase*: this phase determines the collection of all objects whose MBRs satisfy the given query. Since we can not yet determine if these objects satisfy the query, they form the *candidate set*.

2 *refinement phase*: the actual geometry of each member of the candidate set is examined to eliminate false alarms and to find the answer to the query.

The two processing phases are illustrated in Figure 1.5. The filtering phase should be fast and determine the candidates based on the objects' approximations. Since the processing at this stage is performed by means of approximations (e.g., MBRs) the candidate set may contain some *false alarms*. Two simple examples of intersection and containment queries are given in Figure 1.6. If two MBRs intersect each other, this is not necessarily true for the underlying objects (Figure 1.6(a)). Also, if an MBR is totally enclosed by another MBR, then we can not safely judge about the containment of the underlying objects (Figure 1.6(b)).

Although in general the filter step cannot determine the inclusion of an object in the query result, there are few operators (mostly directional ones) that allow for finding query results from the filter step. This is shown in Figure 1.5 by the existence of hits (i.e., answers to the query) in the filter step. The use of a spatial access method provides fast processing of the filter step to discard data objects that can not contribute to the query result.

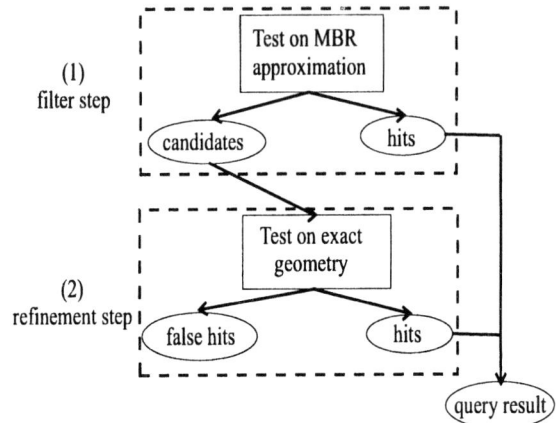

Figure 1.5. Filter-refinement query processing.

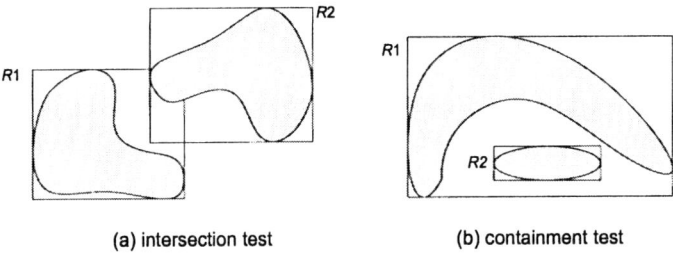

Figure 1.6. Intersection and containment queries.

Among the significant number of spatial access methods that have been proposed in the literature, the R-tree [36] became very popular because of its simplicity, its good average performance and its ability to handle efficiently higher-dimensional data (up to 20 dimensions). R-trees were proposed to solve the indexing problem of rectangles in VLSI design. However, subsequent improvements and enhancements of the basic R-tree structure helped researchers to apply the R-tree successfully in other fields as well (e.g., GIS, multimedia databases). Due to their importance and their wide acceptance, R-trees are presented separately in detail in the next chapter.

4. Handling High-Dimensional Data

In spatial applications data are usually based on two or three dimensions. However, many applications (e.g., multimedia) assume that data are multidimensional, embedded in more dimensions. For example, using the GEMINI approach [28] for indexing multimedia data a time sequence (or time series) can

Spatial Database Concepts

be represented as an N-dimensional vector where N is the number of Discrete Fourier Transform (DFT) coefficients. An example is given in Figure 1.7.

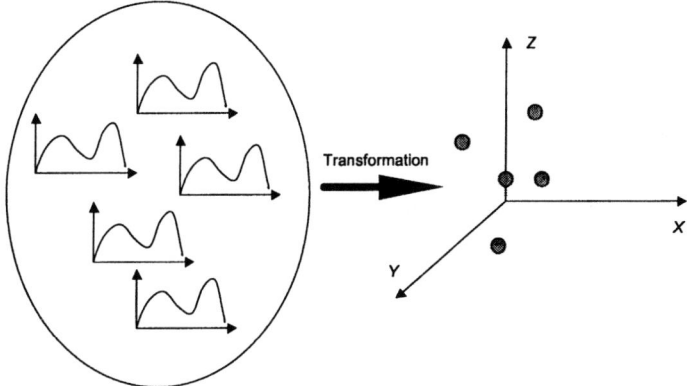

Figure 1.7. Mapping time series to multidimensional vectors.

By using suitable transformations, this technique has been successfully applied for other data types as well (e.g., audio, color images, video). In order to organize these multidimensional vectors a spatial access method can be used. Therefore, we see that even if the original data are not spatial in nature, spatial access methods can still be effectively utilized to organize and efficiently query these datasets.

It has been observed that for very high dimensionalities, most hierarchical spatial access methods degenerate. The reason for this degeneration is twofold:

1. By increasing space dimensionality more space is required to store a single vector, and therefore the index fanout (number of children per node) is reduced considerably resulting in disk accesses increase, and

2. The good properties of index structures do longer hold, since dimensionality increase results in excessive overlap of intermediate nodes, and therefore the discrimination power of the structure is decreased considerably.

Therefore, specialized access methods have been developed to attack the *dimensionality curse* problem. Among the plethora of the proposed multidimesional access methods we note the TV-tree [63], the X-tree [13]. Some of the ideas for NN query processing presented in this book are also applicable to these methods along with the corresponding modifications.

5. Spatial Data Support in Commercial Systems

The support of complex data types (non alphanumeric) and access methods is a key issue in modern database industry, since it allows the DBMS to extend its functionality beyond pure relational data handling. The database industry has performed some very significant steps towards spatial data and spatial query processing support. Among these efforts we highlight the following:

- *Mapinfo SpatialWare*: SpatialWare extends an Informix, Microsoft SQL Server, IBM DB2 or Oracle database to handle spatial data such as points, lines and polygons. It extends database capabilities avoiding a middleware architecture. All functionality is contained directly into the DBMS environment. SpatialWare is implemented in the following ways: 1) in Informix as a *datablade*, 2) in SQL Server using the *extended stored procedure mechanism*, 3) in IBM DB2 as an *extender*, and 4) in Oracle as *spatial server*. SpatialWare provides R-tree support for spatial data indexing purposes [74, 75].

- *Oracle*: Oracle Locator, which is a feature of Oracle Intermedia, provides support for location-based queries in Oracle 9i DBMS. Geographic and location data are integrated in the Oracle 9i server, just like ordinary data types like CHAR and INTEGER. Oracle Spatial provides location-based facilities allowing the extension of Oracle-based applications. It provides data manipulation tools for accessing location information such as road networks, wireless service boundaries, and geocoded customer addresses. Both Oracle Locator and Oracle Spatial provide support for linear quadtrees and R-trees for spatial data indexing purposes [57, 84].

- *IBM Informix and DB2*: In Informix, the R-tree is built-in the database kernel and works directly with the extended spatial data types. The Informix R-tree implementation supports full transaction management, concurrency control, recovery and parallelism. A detailed description of the Informix R-tree implementation can be found in [43]. A description of spatial data handling in a DB2 database can be found in [3].

6. Summary

In order to support applications that require the manipulation of spatial data, the DBMS must be enhanced with additional capabilities regarding data representation, organization, query processing and optimization.

Due to the complexity and volume of spatial datasets, access methods are required to guarantee acceptable query processing performance. Usually, spatial access methods work on object approximation instead of the detailed object spatial characteristics. The most common object approximation is the minimum bounding rectangle (MBR). The use of object approximation is twofold:

1 it helps in discarding a large number of objects without the need for a thorough examination of the detailed spatial characteristics, and

2 it enables the development of efficient and effective access methods. By means of the filter-refinement processing mechanism efficient spatial query processors can be developed.

Taking into consideration that objects in diverse application domains can be modeled as multidimensional points, spatial access methods can be applied in such cases as well. The problem is that with the increase of the space dimensionality, severe problems arise, collectively known as the *dimensionality curse*. Specialized access methods have been proposed to attack this problem.

Due to the importance of spatial data, several commercial systems have already enhanced their products with spatial data manipulation capabilities, enabling the support of geographical information systems and related applications.

7. Further Reading

There are numerous textbooks and monographs that present in detail spatial access methods and spatial query processing. The two books of Samet [111, 112] study in detail spatial access methods and their various applications. Laurini and Thomson in [59] cover several issues regarding spatial access methods and query processing giving emphasis to Geographical Information Systems. Databases issues in Geographical Information Systems are covered in [2]. In [104], Rigaux, Scholl and Voisard perform a thorough study of spatial databases, and cover many important aspects of spatial database systems including modeling, spatial query languages, and query processing. Spatial databases are also covered in detail in a recent book by Shekhar and Chawla [119].

Two very significant introductory research papers for spatial databases have been written by Gueting [35] and Paradaens [98]. Due to the fact that spatial joins and closest-pairs queries are both I/O and CPU intensive, there are many important contributions in the literature [16, 22, 23, 24, 25, 42, 64, 65, 69, 88, 97].

With respect to relevant research papers, one should notice that there is a significant number of sources. For example, all major conferences on databases, such as SIGMOD, VLDB, ICDE, PODS, EDBT and others, have special sessions on the above topics. In addition, there are other more focused conferences, such ACM-GIS, SSD/SSTD, SSDBM, SSTDB and others, where these issues are traditionally discussed.

Chapter 2

THE R-TREE AND VARIATIONS

1. Introduction

In this chapter, we briefly present the R-tree family of spatial access methods, which has been used extensively in research and industry. In fact, many commercial database vendors have adopted the R-tree as a spatial access method to handle spatial objects in their DBMSs.

Since its first application in VLSI design [36], the R-tree has become one of the most popular spatial access methods, and it has been successfully applied to many application domains (e.g., GIS, multimedia databases). Section 2 describes the original R-tree structure. Sections 3 and 4 study briefly dynamic and static R-tree variations. Some performance issues are covered in Section 5, whereas in Section 6 we discuss the adaptation of the structure in emerging applications.

2. The Original R-tree

Although, nowadays the original R-tree is being described in many standard textbooks and monographs on databases [59, 72, 111, 112], we briefly recall its basic properties to make this book self-contained. The R-tree is a hierarchical data structure based on the B^+-tree [52], and it has been proposed as a disk-based access method to organize rectangles. It is used for the dynamic organization of a set of d-dimensional geometric objects representing them by the minimum bounding d-dimensional rectangles (MBRs). Each R-tree node corresponds to the minimum MBR that bounds its children. The tree leaves contain pointers to the database objects, instead of pointers to children nodes. The R-tree nodes are implemented as disk pages.

It must be noted that the MBRs that correspond to different nodes may be overlapping. Besides, an MBR can be included (in the geometrical sense) in many nodes, but can be associated to only one of them. This means that a spatial search may visit many nodes, before confirming the existence or not of a given object MBR. The R-tree has the following fundamental characteristics:

- leaf nodes reside on the same level.

- each leaf contains pairs of the form (R, O), such that R is the MBR that contains spatially object O,

- every internal node contains pairs of the form (R, P), where P is a pointer to a child of the node and R is the MBR that contains spatially the MBRs contained in this child,

- every node (with the possible exception of the root) of an R-tree of class (m, M) contains between m and M pairs, where $m \leq \lceil M/2 \rceil$,

- the root contains at least two pairs, if it is not a leaf.

Figure 2.1 depicts some objects on the left and an example R-tree on the right. Data rectangles R_1 through R_9 are stored in leaf nodes, whereas MBRs R_a, R_b and R_c are hosted at the upper level.

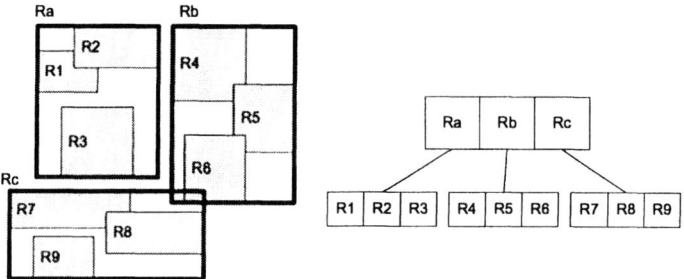

Figure 2.1. An R-tree example.

Insertions of new objects are directed to leaf nodes. At each level, the node that will be least enlarged is chosen. Thus, finally the object is inserted in an existing leaf if there is adequate space, otherwise a split takes place. Adopting as driving criterion the minimization of the sum of the areas of the two resulting nodes, Guttman proposed three alternative algorithms to handle splits, which are of linear, quadratic and exponential complexity:

- *linear split*: Choose two objects as *seeds* for the two nodes, where these objects are as furthest as possible. Then, consider each remaining object in a random order and assign it to the node requiring the smaller enlargement of its respective MBR.

- *quadratic split*: Choose two objects as seeds for the two nodes, where these objects if put together create as much empty space as possible (empty space is the space that remains from the MBR if the areas of the two objects are ignored). Then, until there are no remaining objects, choose for insertion the object for which the difference of empty space if assigned to each of the two nodes is maximized, and insert it in the node that requires smaller enlargement of its respective MBR.
- *exponential split*: All possible groupings are exhaustively tested and the best is chosen with respect to the minimization of the MBR enlargement.

Guttman suggested using the quadratic algorithm as a good compromise between complexity and search efficiency.

In all R-tree variants that have appeared in the literature, tree traversals for any kind of operations are executed in exactly the same way as in the original R-tree. Basically, the R-tree variations differ in the way they handle insertions, and splits during insertions by considering different minimization criteria instead of the sum of the areas of the two resulting nodes. In the sequel, we present the most important dynamic and static R-tree variants.

3. Dynamic R-tree Variants

Here we examine some of the most important dynamic R-tree variants. The methods are characterized *dynamic* since they effectively handle insertions and deletions of data. In the next section we briefly discuss some fundamental *static* R-tree variations, where the data objects must be known in advance.

3.1 The R^+-tree

The R^+-tree was proposed as a structure that avoids visiting multiple paths during point queries and, thus, the retrieval performance could be improved [115, 127]. This is achieved by using the clipping technique. This means that the R^+-tree does not allow overlapping of MBRS at the same tree level. In turn, to achieve this, inserted objects have to be divided in two or more parts, which means that a specific object's entries may be duplicated and redundantly stored in various nodes. Therefore, this redundancy works in the opposite direction of decreasing the retrieval performance in case of window queries. However, the absence of overlap between MBRs in internal nodes improves the overall performance of the structure.

Another side effect of clipping is that during insertions, an MBR augmentation may lead to a series of update operations in a chain-reaction type. Also, under certain circumstances, the structure may lead to a deadlock, as, for example, when a split has to take place at a node with $M+1$ rectangles, where every rectangle encloses a smaller one. An R^+-tree for the same dataset illustrated in Figure 2.1, is presented in Figure 2.2.

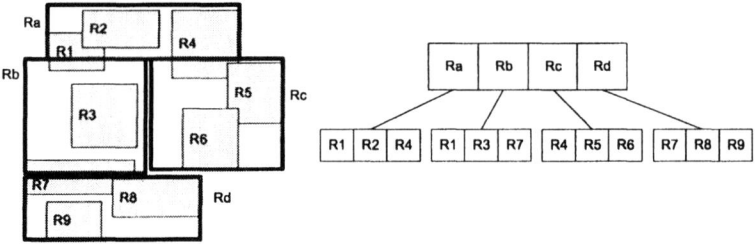

Figure 2.2. An R^+-tree example.

3.2 The R*-tree

Although proposed in 1990 [7], R*-trees are still very well received and widely accepted in the literature as a prevailing performance-wise structure that is often used as a basis for performance comparisons.

The R*-tree does not obey the limitation for the number of pairs per node and follows a sophisticated node split technique. More specifically, the technique of *forced reinsertion* is applied, according to which, when a node overflows, p entries are extracted and reinserted in the tree (p being a parameter, with 30% a suggested optimal value).

Other novel features of R*-trees is that it takes into account additional criteria except the minimization of the sum of the areas of the produced MBRs. These criteria are the minimization of the overlapping between MBRs at the same level, as well as the minimization of the perimeter of the produced MBRs.

Conclusively, the R*-tree insertion algorithm is quite improving in comparison to that of the original R-tree and, thus, improves the latter structure considerably as far as retrievals are concerned (up to 50%). Evidently, the insertion operation is not for free as it is CPU demanding since it applies a *plane-sweep* algorithm [101].

3.3 The Hilbert R-tree

The Hilbert R-tree is a hybrid structure based on R-trees and B^+-trees [50]. Actually, it is a B^+-tree with geometrical objects being characterized by the Hilbert value of their centroid. Thus, leaves and internal nodes are augmented by the largest Hilbert value of their contained objects or their descendants, respectively.

The Hilbert curve is a *space-filling curve*, which can be used to map multidimensional points to the one-dimensional space, by trying to preserve proximity as much as possible. It is desirable, two points close in space to have nearby values, and vice-versa. Other well-known space filling curves are the column-wise curve, the row-wise curve and the Peano curve. Among them it has been shown that the Hilbert curve offers the best performance with respect to proximity preservation [45]. Some space-filling curve examples for the 2-d space are illustrated in Figure 2.3.

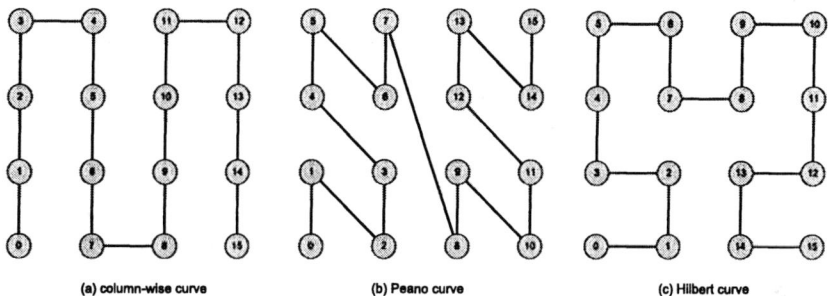

Figure 2.3. Examples of space-filling curves in 2-d space.

For an insertion of a new object, at each level the Hilbert values of the alternative nodes are checked and the smallest one that is larger than the Hilbert value of the object under insertion is followed. In addition, another heuristic used in case of overflow by Hilbert R-trees is the redistribution of objects in sibling nodes. In other words, in such a case up to s siblings are checked to find available space and absorb the new object. A split takes place only if all s siblings are full and, thus, $s+1$ nodes are produced. This heuristic is similar to that applied in B*-trees, where redistribution and 2-to-3 splits are performed during node overflows [52]. According to the authors' experimentation, Hilbert R-trees were proven to be overall the best dynamic version of R-trees as of the time of publication. However, this variant is vulnerable performance-wise to large objects.

4. Static R-tree Variants

There are common applications that use static data. For instance, insertions and deletions in census, cartographic and environmental databases are rare or even they are not performed at all. For such applications, special attention should be paid to construct an optimal structure with regards to some tree characteristics, such as storage overhead minimization, storage utilization maximization, minimization of overlap or cover between tree nodes, or combinations of the above. Therefore, it is anticipated that query processing performance will be improved. These methods are well known in the literature as *packing* or *bulk loading*.

4.1 The Packed R-tree

The first packing algorithm was proposed by Roussopoulos and Leifker in 1985, soon after the proposal of the original R-tree [107]. This first effort basically suggests ordering the objects according to some spatial criterion (e.g., according to ascending x-coordinate) and then grouping them in leaf pages. No experimental work is presented to compare the performance of this method to that of the original R-tree. However, based on this simple inspiration a number of other efforts have been proposed later in the literature.

4.2 The Hilbert Packed R-tree

Kamel and Faloutsos proposed an elaborated method to construct a static R-tree with 100% storage utilization [49]. In particular, among other heuristics they proposed sorting the objects according to the Hilbert value of their centroids and then build the tree in a bottom-up manner.

Experiments showed that the latter method achieves significantly better performance than the original R-tree with quadratic split, the R*-tree and the Packed R-tree by Roussopoulos and Leifker in point and window queries. Moreover, Kamel and Faloutsos proposed a formula to estimate the average number of node access, which is independent of the details of the R-tree maintenance algorithms and can be applied to any R-tree variant.

4.3 The STR Packed R-tree

STR (Sort-Tile-Recursive) is a bulk-loading algorithm for R-trees proposed by Leutenegger et al. in [61]. Let N be a number of rectangles in two-dimensional space. The basic idea of the method is to tile the address space by using S vertical slices, so that each slice contains enough rectangles to create approximately $\sqrt{N/C}$ nodes, where C is the R-tree node capacity.

Initially, the number of leaf nodes is determined, which is $L = \lceil N/C \rceil$. Let $S = \sqrt{L}$. The rectangles are sorted with respect to the x coordinate of the centroids, and S slices are created. Each slice contains $S \cdot C$ rectangles, which are consecutive in the sorted list. In each slice, the objects are sorted by the y coordinate of the centroids and are packed into nodes (placing C objects in a node). The method is applied until all R-tree levels are formulated.

The STR method is easily applicable to high dimensionalities. Experimental evaluation performed in [61] has demonstrated that the STR method is generally better than previously proposed bulk-loading methods. However, in some cases the Hilbert packing approach performs marginally better.

5. Performance Issues

The R-tree and its variations has been successfully applied for range queries, NN queries and spatial join queries. Since all the aforementioned R-tree vari-

The R-tree and Variations

ations have similar hierarchical structures, the query processing techniques are applied without any modification. An exception is the R^+-tree, which uses multiple occurrences of the same object to avoid MBR overlap of the intermediate tree nodes, and therefore duplicate elimination must be applied.

Static variants are generally more efficient than dynamic ones, because the tree structure is more compact, contains fewer nodes and MBR overlap is reduced in comparison to the dynamic case. Since the dataset is known in advance, more effective placement of MBRs to nodes is performed in a static R-tree. In Figure 2.4 the MBRs of the leaf nodes are shown, for three different R-tree variants, namely the R-tree, the R^*-tree and the STR packed R-tree. The dataset used for construction is the hydrography dataset of the Connecticut State, taken from TIGER [138]. Evidently, the STR packed R-tree generates MBRs with less overlap than the other methods.

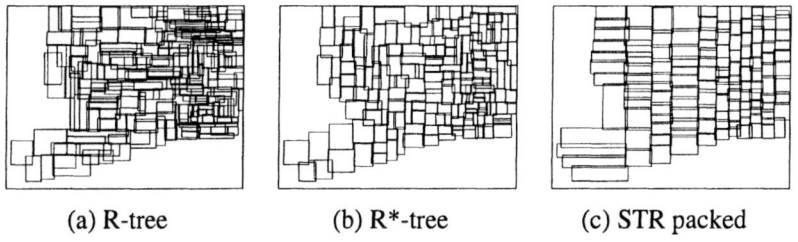

(a) R-tree   (b) R^*-tree   (c) STR packed

Figure 2.4. MBRs of leaf nodes for R-tree, R^*-tree and STR packed R-tree.

Although the R-tree does not guarantee a lower bound with respect to the number of disk accesses required, the average performance is very good, as many experimental results that appeared in the literature have shown. Moreover, the R-tree structure paved the way for the development of efficient spatiotemporal access methods, like the 3-d R-tree [137], Historical R-trees [81, 82] and the Time-Parameterized R-tree (TPR-tree) [110] which have been proposed for spatiotemporal range, NN and join queries. The use of the TPR-tree for NN query processing in moving objects is studied in detail in Chapter 5.

6. R-trees in Emerging Applications

R-trees have not only been used for storing and processing spatial or spatiotemporal data. Modifications to the R-tree structure have been also proposed to speed-up operations in OLAP applications, data warehouses and data mining.

Variations for OLAP and Data Warehouses store summary information in internal nodes, and therefore in many cases it is not necessary to search lower tree levels. Examples of such queries are window aggregate queries, where dataspace parts that satisfy certain aggregate constraints are requested. Nodes totally contained by the query window do not have to be accessed. One of the first efforts in this context is the Ra*-tree variant, which has been proposed for efficient processing of window aggregate queries, where summarized data are stored in internal nodes in addition to the MBR [46]. The same technique has been used in [89] in the case of spatial data warehouses. In [132] the aP-tree has been introduced to process aggregate queries on planar point data. Finally, in [90] a combination of aggregate R-trees and B-trees has been proposed for spatiotemporal data warehouse indexing.

Recently, R-trees have been also used in the context of data mining. In particular, Spatial Data Mining systems [38] include methods that gradually refine spatial predicates, based on indexes like the R-tree, to derive spatial patterns, e.g., spatial association rules [55]. Nanopoulos et al. [78], based on the R-tree structure and the closest-pairs query, developed the C^2P algorithm for efficient clustering, whereas [79] proposed a density biased sampling algorithm from R-trees, which performs effective pre-processing to clustering algorithms.

7. Summary

The R-tree structure has been proposed in 1984 by Guttman to efficiently manipulate rectangles in VLSI chip design. This work influenced many researchers towards the application of the structure for other purposes as well. During the last twenty years many variations of the original structure have been proposed to either improve the performance of spatial queries, or to enable the application of the structure to different contexts. Among the most widely accepted R-tree variants are the R^+-tree, the R*-tree and the Hilbert R-tree. If the dataset is known in advance, more efficient (static) structures can be constructed resulting in considerable performance improvement. The query processing capabilities of the structure have been thoroughly studied in the literature, resulting in efficient algorithms for spatial and spatiotemporal query processing. Recently, the structure has been adopted for query processing purposes in emerging application domains such as OLAP, data warehouses and data mining.

8. Further Reading

In [72] the authors study advanced indexing techniques, including spatial and spatiotemporal access methods. An excellent survey on multidimensional access methods can be found in [34], where several R-tree variants are studied and a very useful classification of access methods is performed. Other access methods that are based on the concepts of the R-tree but use different techniques to group objects include the SS-tree [142] and the SR-tree [51]. Several access methods have been proposed to attack the dimensionality curse problem, such as the TV-tree [63], the X-tree [13] and the A-tree [109]. A recent detailed survey for R-trees and variations including query processing techniques can be found in [73].

II

NEAREST NEIGHBOR SEARCH IN SPATIAL AND SPATIOTEMPORAL DATABASES

Chapter 3

NEAREST NEIGHBOR QUERIES

1. Introduction

In this chapter we present the NN problem and discuss its applications. Although NNN queries have been studied for many different access methods, we focus on the R-tree family. The query processing algorithms are also applied to other access methods with the appropriate modifications.

The structure of the chapter has as follows. In the next section we give the basic definitions of the problem, whereas in Section 3 we discuss its applications. Section 4 presents NN query processing in the R-tree access method. Section 5 discusses important issues of NN search in multimedia database systems.

2. The Nearest Neighbor Problem

Assume that the database is composed of N objects $O_1, O_2, ..., O_N$. Given a query object O_q (which may be contained in the database or not) the NN query asks for the object $O_{nn} \neq O_q$ which is closer to O_q than any other object in the database. A more general form of the query is to ask for the k nearest objects instead of just the closest one. Therefore, the k-NN query asks for the k database objects that are closer to O_q. The output of a k-NN query is a list of objects sorted in increasing distance order from the query object.

Since the NN query retrieves answers according to the proximity of the objects, a distance metric is required. Two of the most common used distance metrics are the Euclidean distance (L_2), and the Manhattan distance (L_1). However, any L_p norm can be applied, as long as the NN processing algorithm takes into consideration the corresponding distance. Given two multidimensional vectors x and y with n dimensions, their L_p distance is defined as follows:

$$L_p(x,y) = \left(\sum_{j=1}^{n} |x_j - y_j|^p \right)^{1/p}$$

where x_j, y_j are the coordinates of the j-th dimension for x and y respectively. Figure 3.1 illustrates examples of 2-NN and 4-NN queries, for a fixed query object, using the L_2 norm (Euclidean). The database objects and the query object are vectors (points) in the 2-d space.

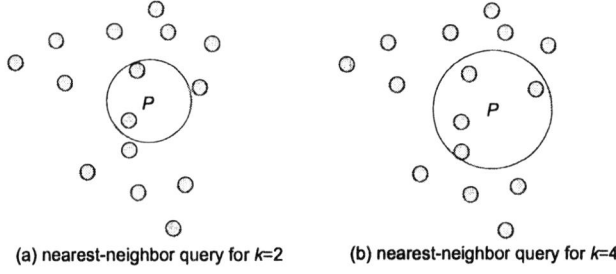

(a) nearest-neighbor query for k=2   (b) nearest-neighbor query for k=4

Figure 3.1. Examples of 2-NN and 4-NN queries using the L_2 norm.

The similarity between the range query and the NN query is obvious. However, in a range query we know exactly the maximum possible distance to a database object, whereas the number of objects that satisfy the answer is not known in advance. On the other hand, in an NN query, we specify the number of objects that will be contained in the answer, but the distance to the furthest object is not known in advance.

Based on the above observation, one could think that a k-NN query could be answered by using repetitive range queries. However, the prediction of the distance is not straightforward. For example, consider the 2-d dataset depicted in Figure 3.2, where we are asking for the three nearest neighbors of point P. The target is to determine the three nearest neighbors of P by performing range queries. However, as it is shown in Figure 3.2, the first three attempts lead to three range queries with radius d_1, d_2 and d_3 respectively. Since no result is returned, the search distance is increased even more to obtain at least three objects. However, the circle with center P and radius d_4 contain much more than three objects, leading to significant performance degradation. In summary, repetitive range queries can lead to either absence of results, or the return of excessive objects. Both cases should be avoided, by using more efficient algorithms for k-NN processing.

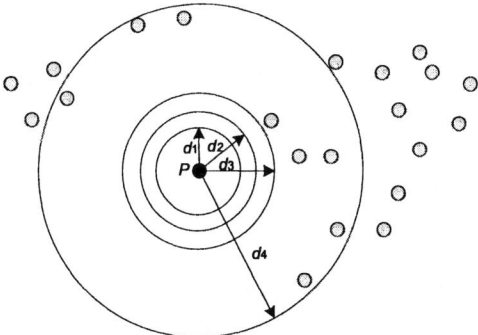

Figure 3.2. Answering a 3-NN query by using repetitive range queries.

3. Applications

NN queries are successfully applied to numerous application domains in diverse fields. Perhaps the most intuitive use of NN queries is in Geographical Information Systems (GIS) where a user may request the five closest cities with respect to a location on a map, or the three nearest hospitals from a car accident location. These queries are intuitive because the object location contains a clear meaning to the user.

In several application domains, database objects are far more complex and rich in content. For example, an image database may contain several thousands of color images, and a user may query the database according to some image characteristics. Consider the query "*retrieve all images that are similar to image Q*" or the query "*retrieve the five images that have similar colors with image Q*". In the above examples, the user must have a clear meaning of the similarity between two images. Similarity in image databases can be expressed by means of color, texture, shape or other image characteristics [83]. Similar queries can be posed for other multimedia types as well, such as audio and video [68].

In the aforementioned applications, NN queries can be applied to determine the similarity between database objects. Since complex objects can be transformed to multidimensional vectors, NN processing can be performed on the transformed space and then the original space is used to discard false alarms and refine the retrieved objects (candidates). An important issue here is the selected distance metric that will be used to express the similarity or the dissimilarity of objects. Usually, the L_2 or the weighted L_2 distance give satisfactory results, but other metrics could be used according to the physical characteristics of the objects.

Since NN queries are applied to determine similar objects, they are also called *similarity queries*. However, range and join queries can also be applied for similarity purposes as well. In a similarity range query we give a query object Q and a distance e and we require all objects that are similar to Q and the dissimilarity (distance) is less than e. For example, the query: *"retrieve all images that are similar to Q, and their dissimilarity with respect to Q is less that e"* is a similarity range query. The similarity join query is basically a join query with the characteristic that the predicate used is related to object similarity between two sets of objects. For example, the query: *"retrieve all pairs of images (x,y) with $x \in X$ and $y \in Y$ such that the dissimilarity between x and y is at most e"*.

As long as the objects can be represented as multidimensional vectors there is no particular difficulty in NN query processing. However, in some applications, objects can not be directly mapped to a multidimensional space, and the only information at hand is the pairwise distance between the objects. For example, in DNA sequences, the distance between sequence A and sequence B can be expressed by means of the *edit distance*, giving the number of modifications required in one sequence to become identical to the other. In such cases there are two approaches that can be followed to process NN queries efficiently:

- specialized access methods, such as M-trees [21] and Slim-trees [139, 140], can be constructed to organize the database objects and provide the required techniques for query processing,

- algorithms, such as FastMap [30], can be applied to map objects to a hypothetical multidimensional space, taking into consideration the distances among the objects. Then, NN queries are easily supported, by using spatial access methods.

Both techniques have been successfully applied in several application domains. The great advantage of the second approach is that after the transformation, multidimensional access methods can be used to organize the objects. On the other hand, the first approach requires specialized access methods and query processing is guided by the *metric space properties*. For any objects O_i and O_j, if $D(O_i, O_j)$ is their distance, then for a metric space the following properties hold:

1 $D(O_i, O_j) \geq 0$ (positivity)

2 $D(O_i, O_j) = D(O_j, O_i)$ (symmetry)

3 $D(O_i, O_j) \leq D(O_i, O_k) + D(O_k, O_j)$ (triangular inequality)

In this book we focus on the vector representation of objects and rely on multidimensional access methods for indexing and retrieval.

4. Nearest Neighbor Queries in R-trees

A very simple method for NN query processing is to search sequentially all database objects, keeping a list of the k nearest neighbors determined. Ev-

Nearest Neighbor Queries

idently, this approach is both I/O and CPU intensive, since the number of database objects is usually very large. Therefore, several algorithms have been reported in the literature aiming at efficient processing of k-NN queries, exploiting the good properties of index structures to reduce both the number of disk accesses and the required processing time. During the search process, several objects are discarded if it is not possible to be part of the final answer.

The first reported algorithm for NN query processing in R-trees has been proposed in [106], which is a modification of the algorithm reported in [33] for the k-d-tree. In order to find the nearest neighbor of a point, the algorithm starts form the R-tree root and proceeds downwards. The key idea of the algorithm is that many branches of the tree can be discarded according to some rules. Two basic distances are defined in n−d space, between a point P with coordinates $(p_1, p_2, ..., p_n)$ and a rectangle R with corners $(s_1, s_2, ..., s_n)$ and $(t_1, t_2, ..., t_n)$ (bottom-left and top-right respectively). These distances are defined as follows:

Definition 3.1
The distance $MINDIST(P, R)$ of a point P from a rectangle R, is defined as follows:

$$MINDIST(P, R) = \sqrt{\sum_{j=1}^{n} |p_j - r_j|^2}$$

where:

$$r_j = \begin{cases} s_j, & p_j < s_j \\ t_j, & p_j > t_j \\ p_j, & \text{otherwise} \end{cases}$$

□

Definition 3.2
The distance $MINMAXDIST(P, R)$ of a point P from a rectangle R, is defined as follows:

$$MINMAXDIST(P, R) = \sqrt{\min_{1 \leq k \leq n} \left(|p_k - rm_k|^2 + \sum_{1 \leq j \leq n, j \neq k} |p_j - rM_j|^2 \right)}$$

where:

$$rm_k = \begin{cases} s_k, & p_k \leq \frac{s_k + t_k}{2} \\ t_k, & \text{otherwise} \end{cases}$$

$$rM_j = \begin{cases} s_j, & p_j \geq \frac{s_j + t_j}{2} \\ t_j, & \text{otherwise} \end{cases}$$

□

Clearly the $MINDIST$ is the optimistic metric, since it is the minimum possible distance that the nearest neighbor of the query point P can reside in the corresponding data page. On the other hand, $MINMAXDIST$ is the pessimistic metric since it is the furthest possible distance where the nearest neighbor of P can reside in the current data page. Therefore, the latter metric guarantees that the nearest neighbors of P lies in a distance not greater than $MINMAXDIST$. The above definitions are shown graphically in Figure 3.3.

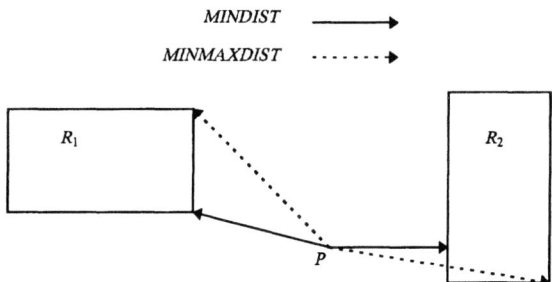

Figure 3.3. MINDIST and MINMAXDIST between a point P and two rectangles R_1 and R_2.

The three basic rules used for pruning the search in the R-tree during traversal follow. Notice that these rules are applied only if one nearest neighbor is required.

Rule 1
If an MBR R has $MINDIST(P, R)$ greater than $MINMAXDIST(P, R')$ of another MBR R', **then** it is discarded because it cannot enclose the nearest neighbor of P.

Rule 2
If an actual distance d from P to a given object is greater than $MINMAXDIST(P, R)$ from P to an MBR R, **then** d is replaced by $MINMAXDIST(P, R)$ because R contains at least one object which is closer to P.

Rule 3
If d_{cur} is the current minimum distance, **then** all MBRs R_j with $MINDIST(P, R_j) > d_{cur}$ are discarded, because they cannot enclose the nearest neighbor of P.

Upon visiting an internal tree node, *Rule 1* and *Rule 2* are used to discard irrelevant branches. Then, a branch is selected according to a priority order. Roussopoulos et al. suggest that when the overlap is small, the $MINDIST$ order should be used since it would discard more candidates. This is also verified in the experimental results of their work. Therefore, the branch which correspond to the minimum $MINDIST$ among all node entries is chosen.

Upon returning from the subtree processing, *Rule 3* is applied to discard other candidates (if there are any). The corresponding algorithm is illustrated in Figure 3.4.

Algorithm NNSearch(Node, Point, Nearest)
1. **if** Node.type == LEAF
2.   **for** i=1 **to** Node.count
3.   dist = objectDIST(Point, Node.branch[i].rect)
4.   **if** dist < Nearest.dist
5.   Nearest.dist = dist
6.   Nearest.rect = Node.branch[i].rect
7.   **endif**
8.   **endfor**
9. **else**
10.   genBranchList(branchList)
11.   sortBranchList(branchList)
12.   last = pruneBranchList(Node, Point, Nearest, branchList)
13.   **for** i = 1 **to** last
14.   newNode = Node.branch[branchList[i]]
15.   NNSearch(newNode, Point, Nearest)
16.   last = pruneBranchList(Node, Point, Nearest, branchList)
17.   **endfor**
18. **endif**
19. **end**

Figure 3.4. NN search algorithm for R-trees.

NN queries in the R^+-tree have been studied by Belussi et al. [8]. Recall that in the R^+-tree no overlap is allowed between nodes in intermediate levels, resulting in object clipping. Therefore, an object may be split to two or more parts to respect the above requirement. Their method considers information on the reference space to improve the search. The resulting data structure integrates the R^+-tree with a regular grid, indexed by using a hashing technique, combining the advantages of the rectangular space decomposition attained by R^+-trees, with a direct access attained by hashing.

5. Nearest Neighbor Queries in Multimedia Applications

In several applications, a transformation is applied to the original objects to obtain a more convenient representation. This technique is ubiquitous to apply efficient indexing schemes for fast query processing, and is applied extensively in multimedia databases. However, the fundamental R-tree NN query processing method presented in the previous section must me adapted accordingly. The main reason for this modification is the avoidance of *false dismissals*, which are objects that satisfy the query constraints but are not retrieved by the search method. Note that although false alarms are allowed (because they can be eliminated in the refinement step), false dismissals result in information loss and therefore they must be avoided.

Let $D(O_1, O_2)$ be the distance between two objects in the original space, and $d(o_1, o_2)$ be the distance of the objects in the transformed space. In order to guarantee the avoidance of false dismissals, D and d must satisfy the following inequality as it has been proven in [5]:

$$d(o_1, o_2) \leq D(O_1, O_2) \qquad (3.1)$$

We assume that our database is composed of a number of audio files, where each one has been sampled with the same rate, and all have equal duration. Our target is, given an audio file, to determine the k audio files that are closer to the query, with respect to the Euclidean distance. Although there are several methods proposed to attack this problem, we focus on a simple technique to illustrate the impact of transformations to the NN search algorithm. Since the original data are too complex to be handled by an indexing scheme, we transform each audio file to the frequency domain by applying the Discrete Fourier Transform (DFT). Then, we keep only the first few DFT coefficients in order to represent each audio file as a point in a multidimensional space. This enables the use of R-trees (or any other multidimensional access method) to index the multidimensional points.

For instance, assume that the audio files are transformed to points in the 2-d space, by the above transformation mechanism. First, we discuss the processing of range queries and the application of the filter-refinement processing paradigm. Next, NN queries are discussed. Given a query audio Q and a non-negative real number e the range query asks for all audio files that lie in at most e distance from Q. Query processing begins from the R-tree that has been built on the transformed objects. The query audio Q must be also transformed by using the same transformation method applied to the data objects. Therefore, a multidimensional point q is derived from the query audio Q. Using q and e the R-tree is searched and let $o_1, o_2, ..., o_n$ be the n multidimensional points that lie inside the circle with radius e centered at q. Because of Equation 3.1, some of the retrieved objects are false alarms and are not part of the final answer. Therefore, by examining the original characteristics of the data objects $O_1, ..., O_n$ false alarms are discarded.

Searching for the k nearest neighbors of a query audio file Q is a bit more complicated than range search. Again, let q be the transformed query and k the

Nearest Neighbor Queries

requested number of nearest neighbors. The basic algorithm is comprised of the following steps:

1. The R-tree is searched to determine the k objects $o_1, ..., o_k$ that are the nearest neighbors of q in the transformed space. Since the retrieved objects may not be the nearest neighbors of Q in the original space, further processing is required.

2. Let o_m, where $1 \leq m \leq k$, be one of the retrieved multidimensional points such that O_m is the furthest from q among the retrieved candidates. The distance $D(Q, O_m)$ is determined between Q and O_m in the original space. Evidently, $d(q, o_m) \leq D(Q, O_m)$ because of Equation 3.1. Using $D(Q, O_m)$ as the radius, a range query is performed centered at q by searching the R-tree, and a new set of r candidates is retrieved, where $k \leq r$.

3. The final set of objects is determined by inspecting the new set of candidates and selecting the k amongst them that are closer to the query object.

We see that the k-NN algorithm contains a step that involves a range query. This is necessary, since the retrieval of the k nearest neighbors in the transformed space does not guarantee that all relevant objects have been found. This happens because the distance between two objects in the transformed space is lower than their corresponding distance in the original space. Therefore, the nearest neighbors in the transformed space may not correspond to the real nearest neighbors of the query object.

ID	rank in original space	rank in transformed space	$D(Q,O)$	$d(q,o)$
ID1	1	1	10	9
ID2	5	2	50	12
ID3	2	3	15	15
ID4	3	4	20	18
ID5	4	5	30	20
ID6	6	6	70	50

Table 3.1. Distances between a query object and some data objects.

This is illustrated in Table 3.1, where the distance between a query object and six database objects is depicted for the original and the transformed space. It is clear that the three nearest neighbors of the query object in the transformed space are ID1, ID2 and ID3 with distances 9, 12 and 15 respectively. However, the three nearest neighbors in the original space are objects ID1, ID3 and ID4. If we rely on the nearest neighbors in the transformed space, object ID4 is lost, and therefore the final result is not correct (we have false dismissals). On the other hand, if we proceed with steps 2 and 3 described above, then the answers are retrieved correctly. From the three candidates retrieved, object ID2 gives the maximum distance in the original space from the query point (i.e. 50). The range query with radius 50 in the transformed space retrieves the objects ID1, ID2, ID3, ID4 and ID5. Finally, by inspecting the distances of these objects from the query object in the original space, we conclude that the final answer is composed by objects ID1, ID3 and ID4.

6. Summary

k-NN queries are extensively used in spatial, spatiotemporal and multimedia database systems. Due to their importance, several query processing algorithms have been developed for various access methods to provide fast retrieval of the answers.

The difficulty in k-NN query processing is that the distance to the k-th nearest object is not known in advance, and therefore an ordinary range query can not be applied. The first proposed k-NN processing algorithm for the R-tree access method has been published in [106].

The algorithm is based on the branch-and-bound technique and on a set of rules that are used to discard irrelevant tree branches. The algorithm can be applied to other hierarchical access methods as well, with minor modifications.

In several cases (especially in databases with complex objects), data objects are transformed to another space to ease the indexing mechanism and therefore allow for more efficient object retrieval during queries. In order to process k-NN queries a few modifications are required to the fundamental algorithm, to avoid false dismissals. The modified algorithm is composed by a) an ordinary k-NN search in the transformed space, b) a range search, and c) a final refinement step to discard false alarms.

7. Further Reading

The complete description of the examined k-NN algorithm for R-trees can be found in [106], where the authors present the algorithm in detail and provide performance evaluation results. In [114] a multistep k-NN search is proposed to provide efficient processing of NN queries in multimedia database systems.

Reverse NN queries determine the set of database objects that have the query point as the nearest neighbor. The reverse and the nearest neighbor problems are asymmetric. If the nearest neighbor of a query point P is a data point Q, then it does not hold in general that P is the nearest neighbor of Q (i.e., P is not necessarily the reverse nearest neighbor). The aforementioned problem has been introduced in [56], however it was restricted to static data and specialized data structures. Stanoi et al. [125] have developed a reverse NN algorithm for the R-tree, which can handle dynamic data efficiently. Recently, Tao, Papadias and Lian have studied the problem for high-dimensional spaces [134].

Hjaltason and Samet [40] presented the problem of *incremental NN searching* with an R-tree. An incremental k-NN query determines the data objects in their order of distance from the query object (*ranking*). In this method the variable k is not necessary to be given in advance, and the user is able to request more nearest neighbors, avoiding the recomputation costs.

Similarity range queries in the context of image databases are studied in [83]. In [5, 31] similarity range queries in time-series are investigated, where the R-tree is used to index time-series data. Query processing techniques and access methods for similarity join queries are studied in [14, 121]. Efficient algorithms and performance evaluation for closest-pair query processing can be found in [22, 23, 24, 25].

Chapter 4

ANALYSIS OF NEAREST NEIGHBOR QUERIES

1. Introduction

An important aspect in database systems is the ability to predict or estimate the cost of the various operations, before their execution. This information can be exploited by query optimizers towards efficient *query execution plan* (QEP) generation. Complex queries (involving selections and joins from several database tables) can be executed in many different ways. The determination of the best query execution plan is not a trivial task, requiring additional knowledge regarding the data distribution, the query distribution, the selectivity of an operator, the index availability, and many more.

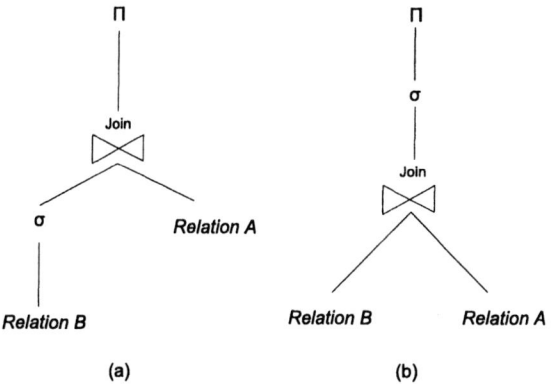

Figure 4.1. Two equivalent query execution plans.

As an example, consider the two different query execution plans depicted in Figure 4.1. Both QEPs, retrieve the same answer, although by using different operator ordering. The first QEP first performs the join operator and then selection is applied. The second QEP first performs the selection and then processes the join. Although both QEPs are equivalent with respect to the answer, their corresponding execution cost may be considerably different.

In this chapter, we study the estimation of the number of disk accesses for the R-tree leaf level for 1-NN queries. More specifically, lower and upper bounds are derived giving the minimum and maximum number of leaf accesses for the processing of 1-NN queries. In order to achieve this goal, the concept of *fractal dimension* is used. The fractal dimension is a very powerful tool that can be used to describe the *data skew* of a dataset. It has been successfully applied for range and join queries [9, 102]. Here, we focus on 1-NN queries and we assume that the underlying R-tree has been constructed by an effective packing method to guarantee the good properties of the structure.

The material of this chapter is based on [93] and is organized as follows. In Section 2 we give the analytical considerations regarding the performance estimation of 1-NN queries, whereas Section 3 contains experimental results comparing the real and the estimated number of disk accesses for 1-NN query processing on R-trees.

2. Analytical Considerations

2.1 Preliminaries

In this section, we derive lower and upper bounds for the performance of the branch-and-bound algorithm. We are interested in the estimation of the number of disk accesses to R-tree leaf pages, because in general the upper levels occupy small space in comparison to the leaf level, and therefore can fit in main memory. The basic notations are presented in Table 4.1.

Assume that the dataspace is composed of a set of points S in the 2-d space. The problem is, given a point $P(p_1, p_2) \in S$, to find its NN point $Q(q_1, q_2)$. Let d_{nn} be the actual Euclidean distance between the points P and Q. The following propositions hold:

Proposition 4.1
The minimum number of leaf pages touched is the number of leaf pages intersected by the circle C_1 with center P and radius d_{nn}.

Proof
The distance d_{nn} is not known in advance. Therefore, even if the nearest neighbor of the query point is found, the algorithm does not stop until all candidates are examined. As a consequence, all data pages X_i with $MINDIST(P, X_i) \leq d_{nn}$ must be searched. $\square$

Analysis of Nearest Neighbor Queries

Symbol	Description
S	a set of 2-d points
N	population of the indexed dataset
n	space dimensionality
σ	side of the square-like data page MBR
D_0	*Hausdorff* fractal dimension
D_2	*correlation* fractal dimension
C_{max}	maximum number of objects per node
C_{avg}	average number of objects per node
U_{avg}	average space utilization
d_{nn}	distance between a query point and its NN point
d_m	distance from a query point to the $MINMAXDIST$ vertex of the first retrieved data page)
q	query window side
$L(q)$	number of leaf accesses for a window query of side q
L_{bound}	lower bound for the number of leaf accesses
U_{bound}	upper bound for the number of leaf accesses

Table 4.1. Basic notations used throughout the analysis.

Before stating Proposition 4.2, we introduce the following basic assumption which is a reasonable property of the algorithm, when the tree nodes have no or very little empty space:

Basic Assumption
The first data page that the algorithm visits, is the data page with the minimum $MINDIST$ among all data pages. □

Proposition 4.2
The maximum number of leaf pages touched is the number of leaf pages that the circle C_2 with center P and radius d_m intersects, where d_m is the $MINMAXDIST$ between P and the first touched leaf page.

Proof
Let R denote the first visited data page MBR. Clearly, the distance $MINMAX$-$DIST(P, R)$ is the maximum possible "safe" distance where a nearest neighbor can be found in this data page. Moreover, it is possible that all data pages X_i with $MINDIST(P, X_i) \leq MINMAXDIST(P, R)$ will be visited, if a particular visiting sequence occurs. □

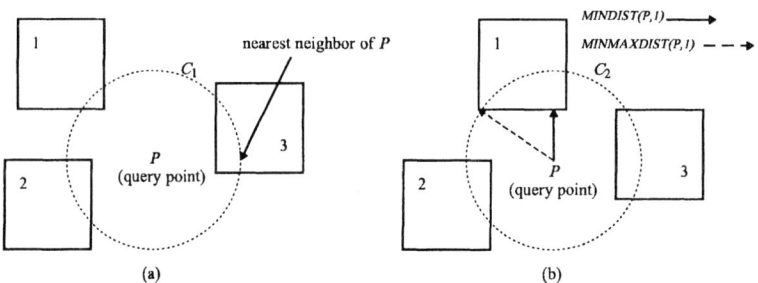

Figure 4.2. (a): example of Proposition 4.1, (b): example of Proposition 4.2.

In Figure 4.2(a) an example is illustrated for Proposition 4.1. The arrow points to the nearest neighbor of the query point P. Even if the algorithm reaches this point, it is not known that this is the nearest neighbor of P, until data pages 1 and 2 are examined. In Figure 4.2(b) Proposition 4.2 is explained. Page 1 is the first visited data page. In the worst case the nearest neighbor of P, in this page, resides in $MINMAXDIST(P, 1)$ from P. However, it is not guaranteed that pages 2 and 3 will be visited. This will occur in the worst case only, and depends on the visiting sequence and the location of the "temporary" NN point in each data page.

The above propositions give a lower bound (Proposition 4.1) and an upper bound (Proposition 4.2) for the number of leaf nodes touched by the algorithm, on the average. We note the importance of the distance d_{nn}, which is the expected distance from P to its nearest neighbor. Therefore, if we had an estimation for d_{nn}, we could provide estimations for the best and worst performance of NN queries. The following subsection deals with the estimation of d_{nn} and d_m.

2.2 Estimation of d_{nn} and d_m

We are interested in the estimation of d_{nn} for arbitrary object distributions. Real datasets show a clear divergence from the uniformity and independence assumption [29] and, therefore, it is better to consider uniformity as a special case. In [9] a formula has been reported that estimates the average number of neighbors $nb(\epsilon, shape)$ of a point P within distance ϵ from P, using the concept

Analysis of Nearest Neighbor Queries

of the *correlation* fractal dimension of the point set:

$$nb(\epsilon, shape) = \left(\frac{volume(\epsilon, shape)}{volume(\epsilon, rect)}\right)^{D_2/n} \cdot (N-1) \cdot 2^{D_2} \cdot \epsilon^{D_2} \quad (4.1)$$

where N is the dataset population, D_2 is the correlation fractal dimension, n is the dataspace dimensionality (2 in our case), and *shape* is the shape with its center of gravity on a point P of the dataset. Since we are interested in NN queries with respect to the Euclidean distance, it is sufficient to set *shape* = *circle*. Making the appropriate modifications in Equation (1) we get:

$$nb(\epsilon, circle) = \left(\frac{\pi\epsilon^2}{4\epsilon^2}\right)^{D_2/2} \cdot (N-1) \cdot 2^{D_2} \cdot \epsilon^{D_2}$$

By simplifying we get:

$$nb(\epsilon, circle) = (\sqrt{\pi})^{D_2} \cdot (N-1) \cdot \epsilon^{D_2} \quad (4.2)$$

We can use Equation (4.2) to estimate the average distance (d_{nn}) of a point P to its nearest neighbor. We are searching for an ϵ such that $nb(\epsilon, circle) = 1$. After substitution in Equation (4.2) and algebraic manipulations we reach:

$$d_{nn} = \epsilon = \frac{1}{\sqrt{\pi} \cdot \sqrt[D_2]{(N-1)}} \quad (4.3)$$

The above equation holds for an arbitrary dataset, when we allow queries to land only on data points. The uniformity case is derived by setting $D_2 = 2$.

Let us now try to estimate the distance d_m, which is the minimum $MINMAXDIST$ between the query point P and the first visited data page. We assume that the MBRs of the data pages are squares with side σ. The following proposition holds:

Proposition 4.3
The maximum possible difference between $MINMAXDIST(P, R)$ and $MINDIST(P, R)$ from a query point P to an MBR R is σ.

Proof
This happens when the query point P coincides with a vertex of the MBR R. This is demonstrated in Figure 4.3. As we can see, when the query point P approaches the bottom-right vertex of the MBR, the difference between $MINMAXDIST$ and $MINDIST$ increases. □

Assuming that the nearest neighbor of a query point lies in the half distance (on the average) between the difference of $MINDIST$ and $MINMAXDIST$,

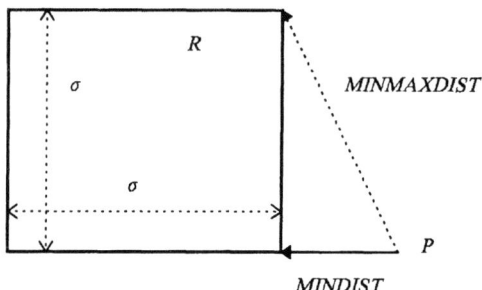

Figure 4.3. When the query point P coincides with a vertex of the MBR, then the maximum difference (σ) between $MINDIST$ and $MINMAXDIST$ is obtained.

we need only to augment d_{nn} by $\sigma/2$ to reach the $MINMAXDIST$. Therefore, we conclude that the distance d_m which gives the upper bound of Proposition 4.2 is calculated by the following equation:

$$d_m = \frac{1}{\sqrt{\pi} \cdot \sqrt[D_2]{(N-1)}} + \frac{\sigma}{2} \qquad (4.4)$$

2.3 Performance Estimation

Let S be a set of N data points distributed in the unit square address space. We are interested in estimating the number of data pages retrieved, when the nearest neighbor is requested for any point $P \in S$. Given a query window $q \times q$, the number of leaf nodes $L(q)$ retrieved is given by a formula reported in [29], which assumes that queries are distributed uniformly on the address space i.e. each dataspace portion has the same probability to be requested:

$$L(q) = \frac{N}{C_{avg}} \cdot (\sigma + q)^2 \qquad (4.5)$$

where $\sigma = \left(\frac{C_{avg}}{N}\right)^{1/D_0}$, $C_{avg} = C_{max} \cdot U_{avg}$, N is the dataset population, D_0 is the *Hausdorff* (box counting) fractal dimension of the underlying point dataset, C_{max} is the maximum node capacity and U_{avg} is the average space utilization of the R-tree nodes.

However, in our case we cannot use Equation (4.5). This is due to the fact, the queries can land only on (existing) data points and therefore at least one leaf access will occur. In other words, in our case the query model assumes that the query distribution follows the data distribution (i.e. each data object has the same probability of retrieval [87]). Therefore, we are going to derive a formula that obeys the latter query model.

Assume we have a $q \times q$ window and we have to perform a range query Q over the underlying address space. We know that the average size of each data

Analysis of Nearest Neighbor Queries

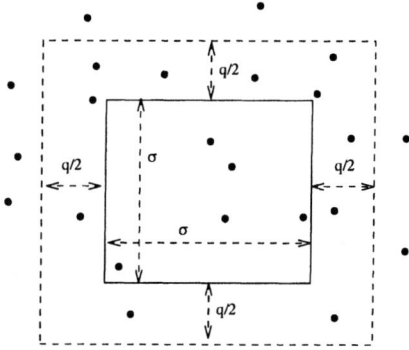

Figure 4.4. Example of an enlarged data page.

page MBR is $\sigma \times \sigma$. We are interested in calculating the probability P_{fetch} that a data page will be fetched due to the execution of Q. A data page will be fetched only if the centroid of the window $q \times q$ falls in the area surrounded by the dashed line of Figure 4.4. Note however, that the query window centroid can only coincide with an existing data point (according to the query model considered in this chapter). Therefore, the probability P_{fetch} can be defined as:

$$P_{fetch} = \frac{GoodPoints}{AllPoints} \qquad (4.6)$$

where $GoodPoints$ is the number of points enclosed by the enlarged $(\sigma + q) \times (\sigma + q)$ window, and $AllPoints$ is the population, N, of the indexed dataset. However, we have the appropriate mathematical tools to calculate $GoodPoints$. We can use Equation (4.1) setting $shape = rect$ and $\epsilon = \frac{\sigma+q}{2}$. This requires an optimistic assumption that we can always find a data point on the data page MBR centroid. Therefore, we have:

$$GoodPoints = (N-1) \cdot (\sigma + q)^{D_2} \qquad (4.7)$$

From Equations (4.6) and (4.7) we get:

$$P_{fetch} = \frac{N-1}{N} \cdot (\sigma + q)^{D_2} \qquad (4.8)$$

Our next step is to calculate the average number of data page accesses. We know that the total number of data pages is $\frac{N}{C_{avg}}$. Therefore:

$$L(q) = \frac{N}{C_{avg}} \cdot P_{fetch} \Rightarrow L(q) = \frac{N-1}{C_{avg}} \cdot (\sigma + q)^{D_2} \qquad (4.9)$$

In order to get the lower and upper bounds for the number of leaf accesses, we must substitute q in Equation (4.9), with $2 \cdot d_{nn}$ from Equation (4.3), and

$2 \cdot d_m$ from Equation (4.4), respectively. Therefore, we have:

$$L_{bound} = \frac{N-1}{C_{avg}} \cdot (\sigma + 2 \cdot d_{nn})^{D_2} \qquad (4.10)$$

$$U_{bound} = \frac{N-1}{C_{avg}} \cdot (\sigma + 2 \cdot d_m)^{D_2} \qquad (4.11)$$

Equations (4.10) and (4.11) include uniformity as a special case. Clearly, for uniform point sets $D_0 \approx 2$ and $D_2 \approx 2$, so we can use the above equations for any kind of point set. Also, we note that L_{bound} and U_{bound} are bounds on the average case and not absolute ones. This means that during NN query processing, the lower bound may be higher than the leaf pages touched. However, we are interested on the average case, and exceptional cases do not harm the generality.

3. Performance Evaluation
3.1 Preliminaries

We implemented the branch-and-bound algorithm [106] and the Hilbert-packed R-tree [49] in the C programming language under UNIX, and ran the experiments on a DEC Alpha 3000 workstation. We used randomly generated as well as real-life points to verify the theoretical aspects. The datasets used are depicted in Figure 4.5. The real-life points are 9,552 road intersections of the Montgomery County, Maryland (MG). For uniform point sets we have $D_0 \approx 2$ and $D_2 \approx 2$, whereas for the MG points $D_0 \approx 1.719$ and $D_2 \approx 1.518$ [9].

Random points   MG points

Figure 4.5. Datasets used in the experiments.

Analysis of Nearest Neighbor Queries 45

3.2 Experimental Results

In all experimental series, for each dataset, the average number of leaf accesses was determined by issuing an NN query for each existing data point. Also, the lower and upper bounds for the average number of leaf accesses were calculated. The measured average number of leaf accesses is shown in the last column of each subsequent table.

Experiment 1

The dataset is composed of a number of uniformly distributed points. The maximum R-tree node capacity was set to 50 objects. In Table 4.2 we present the results for uniform data of various populations.

Experiment 2

The dataset is composed of uniformly distributed points. Here, we keep the dataset population constant at 50,000 and vary the maximum tree fanout from 10 to 200. The results are shown in Table 4.3.

Experiment 3

The dataset is composed of the 9,552 MG points. Again, we vary the tree fanout from 10 to 200 as in Experiment 2. The results are presented in Table 4.4

From these tables it is evident that the lower and upper bounds enclose very well the measured average number of leaf accesses. Therefore, one could use the simple Formulae (4.10) and (4.11) to estimate the performance of an NN query. We observe that the measured number of leaf accesses is generally closer to the lower bound than the upper bound. This gives us a strong indication that the branch-and-bound algorithm with the $MINDIST$ criterion exploits the "*goodness*" property of the packed R-tree very effectively. The lower bound gives an optimistic metric, whereas the upper bound gives a pessimistic metric. Both bounds are valuable in query processing and optimization. Another observation is that when the data (and hence the query) distribution is uniform, the bounds do not depend on the dataset population. This can be verified by substituting the appropriate values for σ, d_{nn} and d_m in Equations (4.10) and (4.11), and is illustrated in Table 4.2.

4. Summary

The cost estimation of NN queries is not a trivial task. In this chapter we have studied an approach which is based on the fractal dimensionality of the dataset. We have focused on point datasets in 2-d space, which are indexed by a well-formed R-tree structure.

We have shown that the actual distance between a point and its nearest neighbor plays a very important role for the performance estimation of NN queries.

Population	Lower	Upper	Measured
1,000	1.34	4.66	1.63
2,000	1.34	4.66	1.58
10,000	1.34	4.66	1.70
20,000	1.34	4.66	1.80
50,000	1.34	4.66	2.04
100,000	1.34	4.66	1.88
200,000	1.34	4.66	2.28
500,000	1.34	4.66	1.97

Table 4.2. Number of leaf accesses vs. data population. Data=Uniform, Fanout=50.

Fanout	Lower	Upper	Measured
5	2.26	6.27	3.02
10	1.84	5.55	2.68
20	1.56	5.07	2.19
50	1.34	4.66	2.03
100	1.23	4.46	1.90
200	1.16	4.32	1.82

Table 4.3. Number of leaf accesses vs. fanout. Data=Uniform, Population=50,000.

Fanout	Lower	Upper	Measured
5	3.22	7.99	4.13
10	2.70	7.01	3.06
20	2.33	6.24	2.36
50	1.98	5.44	2.27
100	1.77	4.94	1.89
200	1.61	4.52	1.81

Table 4.4. Number of leaf accesses vs. fanout. Data=MG points, Population $\approx$ 9,000.

Experiments based on synthetic and real-life data have shown that the derived bounds enclose very closely the number of leaf accesses introduced during the processing of an NN query. In fact, the performance of the branch-and-bound algorithm is closer to the lower bound, and therefore is very efficient. This estimation could be exploited by a query optimizer, to derive an efficient query processing plan.

5. Further Reading

The cost estimation of spatial operators is a very important research field and many important results have been published. Since most database operations are I/O intensive, the number of disk accesses gives an idea about the operation cost. In [9, 29, 87, 135] the authors provide closed-form formulae for the estimation of the number of R-tree node accesses for range queries. In [12, 133] performance estimation of NN queries in multidimensional spaces is studied in detail. Spatial join performance estimation is discussed in [15, 32, 70, 80, 102].

Chapter 5

NEAREST NEIGHBOR QUERIES IN MOVING OBJECTS

1. Introduction

In Chapter 3 we studied NN query processing in stationary datasets (the object locations remain fixed, or change very rarely). In this chapter we focus on spatiotemporal databases, which is an emerging research field. More specifically, we assume that data objects are not stationary, but can change their location in space. NN query processing for moving objects is a challenging research area, since traditional query processing techniques are not very efficient and therefore are not directly applicable.

Spatiotemporal database systems aim at combining the spatial and temporal characteristics of data. There are many applications that benefit from efficient processing of spatiotemporal queries such as: mobile communication systems, traffic control systems (e.g., air-traffic monitoring), geographical information systems, multimedia applications. The common basis of the above applications is the requirement to handle both the space and time characteristics of the underlying data [122, 136, 145]. These applications pose high requirements concerning the data and the operations that need to be supported, and therefore new techniques and tools are needed towards increased processing efficiency.

A moving dataset is composed of objects whose positions change with respect to time (e.g., moving vehicles). Examples of basic queries that could be posed to such a dataset include:

- *range query*: given a region (e.g., a rectangle) R that changes position and size with respect to time, determine the objects that are covered by R from time point t_s to t_e.

- *nearest neighbor query*: given a moving point P determine the k nearest neighbors of P within the time interval $[t_s, t_e]$.

- *join query*: given two moving datasets S_1 and S_2, determine the pairs of objects (s_1, s_2) with $s_1 \in S_1$ and $s_2 \in S_2$ such that s_1 and s_2 overlap at some point in $[t_s, t_e]$.

- *closest-pairs query*: given two moving datasets S_1 and S_2, determine k pairs of objects (s_1, s_2) with $s_1 \in S_1$ and $s_2 \in S_2$ such that their pairwise distance is the smallest amongst all possible pairs for the time interval $[t_s, t_e]$.

Queries that require an answer for a specific time instance (time-slice queries) are special cases of the above examples, and generally are more easily processed. Queries that must be evaluated for a time interval $[t_s, t_e]$ are characterized as *continuous* [123, 131]. In some cases, the query must be evaluated continuously as time advances. The basic characteristic of continuous queries is that there is a change in the answer at specific time points, which must be identified to produce correct results.

Existing methods are either computationally intensive performing repetitive queries to the database, or are restrictive with respect to the application settings (i.e., are applied only for static datasets, or are applicable for special cases that limit the space dimensionality or the requested number of nearest neighbors). The objective of this chapter is twofold:

- to study efficient algorithms for NN query processing on moving object datasets,

- to compare the proposed algorithms with existing methods through an extensive experimental evaluation, by considering several parameters that affect query processing performance.

The chapter is based on [103] and is organized as follows. In Sections 2 and 3 we give the appropriate background and related work for completeness. In Section 4, the proposed approach is studied in detail and the application to TPR-trees is presented. Finally, in Section 5, a performance evaluation of all methods is conducted and the results are interpreted.

2. Organizing Moving Objects

The research conducted in access methods and query processing techniques for moving-object databases are generally categorized in the following areas:

- query processing techniques for past positions of objects, where past positions of moving objects are archived and queried, using multiversion access methods or specialized access methods for object trajectories [66, 81, 100, 129, 146],

- query processing techniques for present and future positions of objects, where each moving object is represented as a function of time, giving

Nearest Neighbor Queries in Moving Objects 51

the ability to determine its future positions according to the current characteristics of the object movement (reference position, velocity vector) [4, 44, 47, 53, 54, 60, 77, 110, 144].

We focus on the second category, where it is assumed that the dataset consists of moving point objects, which are organized by means of a Time-Parameterized R-tree (TPR-tree) [110]. The TPR-tree is an extension of the well known R*-tree [7], designed to handle object movement. Objects are organized in such a way that a set of moving objects is bounded by a moving rectangle to maintain a hierarchical organization of the underlying dataset. The TPR-tree differs from the R*-tree in the following key characteristics:

- bounding rectangles in the TPR-tree internal nodes although are *conservative*, they are not *minimum* in general,

- the TPR-tree is efficient for a time interval $[t_0, H)$, where H (horizon) is the time point which suggests a reorganization, due to extensive overlapping of bounding rectangles.

- all metrics used for insertion, reinsertion and node splitting in the TPR-tree are based on integrals which calculate overlap, enlargement and margin for the time interval $[t_0, H)$,

- TPR-trees answer time-parameterized queries for a given time interval $[t_s, t_e]$, or for a specific time instance.

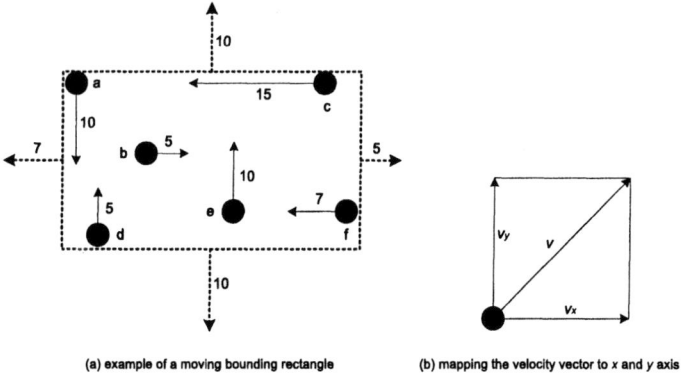

(a) example of a moving bounding rectangle   (b) mapping the velocity vector to x and y axis

Figure 5.1. Generation of a moving bounding rectangle.

Figure 5.1 depicts how a moving bounding rectangle is generated for a set of moving objects in 2-d space. Each object is characterized by its reference position (location) and its velocity vector. If the object movement is not parallel to the x or y axis, the velocity vector is analyzed as it is shown in Figure 5.1(b). The generated moving bounding rectangle is constructed by calculating the MBR for the reference time instance t_0 and by assigning a velocity vector to its four edges, as it is shown in Figure 5.1(a). Bounding rectangles for the upper tree levels are generated similarly.

3. Nearest Neighbor Queries

Allowing the query and the objects to move, an NN query takes the following forms:

- Given a query point reference position P, a query velocity vector v_q, a time point t_x and an integer k, determine the k nearest neighbors of P at t_x (time-slice NN query).

- Given a query point reference position P, a query velocity vector v_q, an integer k and a time interval $[t_1, t_2)$, determine the k nearest neighbors of P according to the query and object movements from t_1 to t_2 (continuous or time-interval NN query).

The second query type is more difficult to answer, since it requires knowledge of specific time instances which indicate that there is a change in the answer set. These time instances are called *split points*.

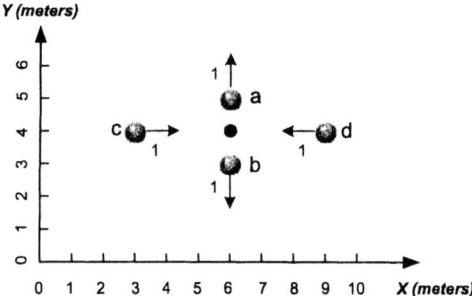

Figure 5.2. A NN query example in a moving dataset.

Figure 5.2 shows an example database of four moving objects. Assume that the k=2 nearest neighbors are requested for the time interval $[0, 5]$. Assume also that the query point is static (black circle). By observing the object movement with respect to the query, it is evident that for the time interval $[0, 2)$ the nearest neighbors of P are b and a, whereas for the time interval $[2, 5)$ the nearest neighbors are c and d. In the sequel, we briefly describe research results towards solving NN queries in moving datasets.

Kollios et al. [53] propose a method able to answer NN queries for moving objects in 1-d space. The method is based on the dual transformation where a line segment in the native space corresponds to a point in the transformed space, and vice-versa. The method determines the object that comes closer to the query between $[t_s, t_e]$ and not the nearest neighbors for every time instance.

Zheng et al. [148] proposed a method for computing a single nearest neighbor ($k = 1$) of a moving query, applied to static points indexed by an R-tree. The method is based on Voronoi diagrams and it seems quite difficult to be extended for other values of k and higher space dimensions.

In [123] a method is presented to answer such queries on moving-query, static-objects cases. Objects are indexed by an R-tree, and sampling is used to query the R-tree at specific points. However, due to the nature of sampling, the method may return incorrect results if a split point is missed. A low sampling rate yields more efficient performance, but increases the probability of incorrect results, whereas a high sampling rate poses unnecessary computational overhead, but decreases the probability of incorrect results.

Benetis et al. [10] propose an algorithm capable of answering NN queries and reverse NN queries in moving-object datasets. The proposed method is restricted in answering only one nearest neighbor per query.

In [131] the authors propose an NN query processing algorithm for moving-query moving-objects, based on the concept of time-parameterized queries. Each query result is composed of the following components: i) R is the current query result set, ii) T is the time point in which the result becomes invalid, and iii) C is the set of objects that influence the result at time T. Therefore, by continuously calculating the next set of objects that will influence the result, we determine the nearest neighbors of the query from t_1 to t_2. A TPR-tree index is used to organize the moving objects.

The main drawback of the aforementioned method is that the TPR-tree is searched several times in order to determine the next object that influences the current result. This implies additional overhead in CPU and I/O time, which is more severe as the number of requested nearest neighbors increases. In [130] the same authors present a method which is applicable for static datasets to overcome the problems of repetitive NN queries. By assuming that the dataset is indexed by an R-tree structure, a single query is performed and therefore each participating tree node is accessed only once. Performance results demonstrate that NN queries are answered much more efficiently concerning query response time. However, the proposed techniques can only be applied for static datasets.

Table 5.1 presents a categorization of NN queries with respect to the characteristics of queries and datasets. There are four different problem versions that are formulated by considering queries and datasets as *static* or *moving*. The table also summarizes the previously mentioned related work for each problem.

In the sequel, we study an efficient algorithm for NN query processing for moving-query moving-object databases, with the following characteristics:

- the method is applied for *any* number of requested nearest neighbors,

Query	Data	Related Work
Static	Static	conventional techniques
Static	Moving	special case of moving-query moving-data
Moving	Static	Roussopoulos et al [123] Zheng et al. [148] Tao et al. [130]
Moving	Moving	Tao et al. [131] Kollios et at. [53] Benetis et al. [10]

Table 5.1. NN queries for different query and data characteristics.

- the method can be applied for *any* number of space dimensions, since only relative distances are computed during query processing,
- different tree pruning algorithms may be applied during tree traversal,
- each tree node is accessed only once, therefore the consumption of system resources is reduced,
- the method not only reports the time instances when there is a change in the result, but also the time instances when there is a change in the order of the nearest neighbors in the current result.

The challenge is to determine the k nearest neighbors of a given moving query point P, a query velocity vector vp and a time interval $[t_s, t_e]$. We want to answer such a query, by performing only one search, thus avoiding posing repetitive queries to the database. The answer to the query is a set of mutually exclusive time intervals, and a sorted list of object IDs for each time interval, which are the k nearest neighbors of P for the respective time interval.

By assuming that the distance between two points is determined by the distance measure, the distance $D_{P,Q}(t)$ between query P and object Q as a function of time is given by the following equation:

$$D_{P,Q}(t) = \sqrt{c_1 \cdot t^2 + c_2 \cdot t + c_3} \qquad (5.1)$$

where c_1, c_2, c_3 are constants given by:

$$c_1 = (vq_x - vp_x)^2 + (vq_y - vp_y)^2$$

Nearest Neighbor Queries in Moving Objects

$$c_2 = 2 \cdot [(Q_x - P_x) \cdot (vq_x - vp_x) + (Q_y - P_y) \cdot (vq_y - vp_y)]$$

$$c_3 = (Q_x - P_x)^2 + (Q_y - P_y)^2$$

vq_x, vq_y are the velocities of object Q, vp_x, vp_y are the query point velocities in each dimension, whereas $(Q_x, Q_y), (P_x, P_y)$ are the reference positions of the object Q and the query P respectively. In the sequel, we assume that the distance is given by $(D_{P,Q}(t))^2$ to perform simpler calculations.

The movement of an object with respect to the query is visualized by plotting the function $(D_{P,Q}(t))^2$, as illustrated in Figure 5.3. For NN query processing the distance from the query point contains all the necessary information, since the exact object position is irrelevant. Note that since $c_1 \geq 0$ the plot of the function always has the shape of a "valley'.

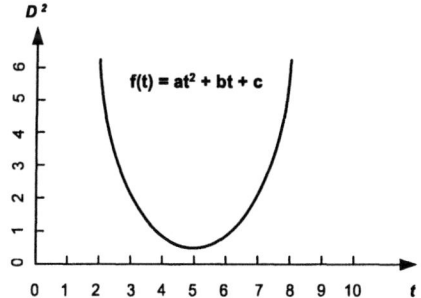

Figure 5.3. Visualization of the distance between a moving object and a moving query.

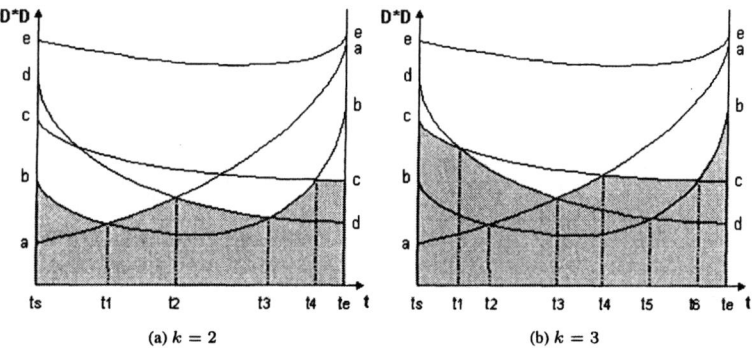

Figure 5.4. Relative distance of objects with respect to a moving query.

Assume that we have a set of moving objects Q and a moving query point P. The objects and the query are represented as points in a multidimensional space.

Although the proposed method can be applied to any number of dimensions, the presentation is restricted to 2-d space for clarity and convenience. Moving queries and objects are characterized by their reference positions and velocity vectors. Therefore, we have all the necessary information to define the distance $(D_{P,Q}(t))^2$ for every object $q \in Q$. By visualizing the relative object movement during $[t_s, t_e]$ a graphical representation is derived, such as the one depicted in Figure 5.4.

By inspecting Figure 5.4 we obtain the k nearest neighbors of the moving query during the time interval $[t_s, t_e]$. For example, for $k = 2$ the nearest neighbors of P for the time interval are contained in the shaded area of Figure 5.4. The nearest neighbors of P for various values of k along with the corresponding time intervals are depicted in Figure 5.5. The pair of objects above each time point t_x declare the objects that have an intersection at t_x. These time points where a modification of the result is performed, are called *split points*. Note that not all intersection points are split points. For example, the intersection of objects a and c in Figure 5.4 is not considered as a split point for $k = 2$, whereas it is a split point for $k = 3$.

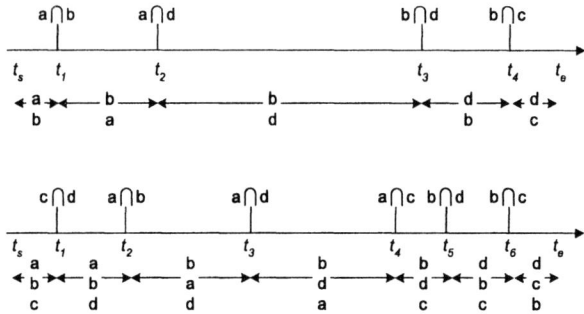

Figure 5.5. Nearest neighbors of the moving query for $k = 2$ (top) and $k = 3$ (bottom).

The previous example demonstrates that the k nearest neighbors of a moving query can be determined by using the functions that represent the distance of each moving object with respect to the moving query. Based on the previous discussion, the next section presents the design of an algorithm for NN query processing (*NNS*) which operates on moving objects.

3.1 The NNS Algorithm

The *NNS* algorithm consists of two parts, which are described separately:

- *NNS-a* algorithm: given a set of moving objects, a moving query and a time interval, the algorithm returns the k nearest neighbors for the given interval, and

- *NNS-b* algorithm: given the k nearest neighbors, the corresponding time intervals, and a new moving object, the algorithm computes the new result.

3.1.1 Algorithm NNS-a

We are given a moving query point P, a set Q of N moving objects, a time interval $[t_s, t_e]$, whereas the k nearest neighbors of P are requested. The target is to partition the time interval into one or more sub-intervals, in which the list of nearest neighbors remains unchanged. Each time sub-interval is defined by two time split points, declaring the beginning and the sub-interval end. During the calculation, the set Q is partitioned into three sub-sets:

- the set $\mathcal{K}$, which always contains k objects that are currently the nearest neighbors of P,

- the set $\mathcal{C}$, which contains objects that are possible candidates for subsequent time points, and

- the set $\mathcal{R}$, which contains rejected objects whose contribution to the answer is impossible for the given time interval $[t_s, t_e]$.

Initially, $\mathcal{K} = \emptyset$, $\mathcal{C} = \mathcal{O}$, and $\mathcal{R} = \emptyset$. The first step is to determine the k nearest neighbors for time point t_s. By inspecting Figure 5.4 for $k = 2$ we get that these objects are a and b. Therefore, $\mathcal{K} = \{a, b\}, \mathcal{C} = \{c, d, e\}$ and $\mathcal{R} = \emptyset$. Next, for each $o \in \mathcal{K}$ the intersections with objects in $\mathcal{K} + \mathcal{C}$ are determined. If there exist any objects in $\mathcal{C}$ that do not intersect any objects in $\mathcal{K}$, they are removed from $\mathcal{C}$ and are put in $\mathcal{R}$, meaning that they will not be considered again (Proposition 5.1). In our example, object e is removed from $\mathcal{C}$ and we have $\mathcal{K} = \{a, b\}, \mathcal{C} = \{c, d\}$ and $\mathcal{R} = \{e\}$. The currently determined intersections are kept in an ordered list, in increasing time order. Each intersection is represented as $(t_x, \{u, v\})$, where t_x is the time point of the intersection and $\{u, v\}$ are the objects that intersect at t_x.

Proposition 5.1
Moving objects that do not intersect the k nearest neighbors of the query at time t_s, can be rejected.

Proof
An intersection between o_1 and o_2 denotes a change in the result. Therefore, if none of the k nearest neighbors intersect any other object between $[t_s, t_e]$, there will be no change in the result. This means that we do not have to consider other objects for determining the nearest neighbors. □

Each intersection is defined by two objects u and v. If three or more objects intersect at the same point t_x the conflict is resolved by evaluating the first derivative for each object at t_x and taking the minimum value. The currently determined intersection points comprise the current list of time split points. According to the example, the split point list has as follows: $(t_1, \{a, b\})$, $(t_2, \{a, d\})$, $(t_x, \{a, c\})$, $(t_3, \{b, d\})$, $(t_4, \{b, c\})$. For each intersection we distinguish between two cases:

- $u \in \mathcal{K}$ and $v \in \mathcal{K}$
- $u \in \mathcal{K}$ and $v \in \mathcal{C}$ (or $u \in \mathcal{C}$ and $v \in \mathcal{K}$)

In the first case, the current set of nearest neighbors does not change. However, the order of the currently determined objects changes, since two objects in $\mathcal{K}$ intersect, and therefore they exchange their position in the ordered list of nearest neighbors. Therefore, objects u and v exchange their position. In the second case, object v is inserted into $\mathcal{K}$ and therefore the list of nearest neighbors must be updated accordingly (Proposition 5.2).

Proposition 5.2
Let us consider a split point at time t_x, at which objects o_1 and o_2 intersect. If $o_1 \in \mathcal{K}$ and $o_2 \in \mathcal{C}$ then at t_x, o_1 is the k-th nearest neighbor of the query.

Proof
Assume that o_1 is not the k-th nearest neighbor at the intersection time. However, o_1 belongs to the result (is among the k nearest neighbors) at time t_x. The intersection at time t_x denotes that objects o_1 and o_2 are consecutive in the result. This implies that o_2 is already contained in the current result (set $\mathcal{K}$) which contradicts our assumption that o_2 is not contained in the result set. Therefore, object o_1 must be the k-th nearest neighbor of the query. □

According to the currently determined split points, the first split point is t_1, where objects a and b intersect. Since both objects are contained in $\mathcal{K}$, no new objects are inserted into $\mathcal{K}$, and simply objects a and b exchange their position. Up to this point concerning the sub-interval $[t_s, t_1)$ the nearest neighbors of P are a and b. We are ready now to check the next split point, t_2, where objects a and d intersect. Since $a \in \mathcal{K}$ and $d \in \mathcal{C}$ object a is removed from $\mathcal{K}$ and inserted into $\mathcal{C}$. On the other hand, object d is removed from $\mathcal{C}$ and inserted into $\mathcal{K}$ taking the position of a. Up to this point, another part of the answer has been determined, since in the sub-interval $[t_1, t_2)$ the nearest neighbors of P are b and a. Moving to the next intersection, t_x, we see that this intersection is caused by objects a and c. However, neither of these objects is contained in $\mathcal{K}$. Therefore, we ignore t_x and remove it from the list of time split points. Since a new object d has been inserted into $\mathcal{K}$, we check for new intersections between d and objects in $\mathcal{K}$ and $\mathcal{C}$. No new intersections are discovered, and therefore we move to the next split point t_3. Currently, for the time sub-interval $[t_2, t_3)$

the nearest neighbors of P are b and d. At t_3 objects b and d intersect, and this causes a position exchange. We move to the next split point t_4 where objects b and c intersect. Therefore, object b is removed from $\mathcal{K}$ and inserted into $\mathcal{C}$, whereas object c is removed from $\mathcal{C}$ and inserted into $\mathcal{K}$. Since c does not have any other intersections with objects in $\mathcal{K}$ and $\mathcal{C}$, the algorithm terminates. The final result is depicted in Figure 5.5, along with the corresponding result for $k = 3$. The method outline is illustrated in Figure 5.6.

Algorithm *NNS-a*
Input: a set of moving objects $\mathcal{O}$, a moving query point P,
time interval $[t_s, t_e]$, the number k of requested NNs
Output: a list of elements of the form $([t_1, t_2], o_1, o_2, ..., o_k)$
where $o_1, ..., o_k$ are the NNs of P from t_1 to t_2 (*CNN-list*),
split-list containing the split points
Local: k-list containing the current NNs
1.   initialize $\mathcal{K} = \emptyset, \mathcal{C} = \mathcal{O}$, and $\mathcal{R} = \emptyset$
2.   initialize *split-list* with split points t_s and t_e
3.   find the k NNs of P at time point t_s
4.   update k-list
5.   **foreach** $u \in \mathcal{K}$ **do**
6.   find intersections with $v \in \mathcal{K}$
7.   find intersections with $v \in \mathcal{C}$
8.   update split list
9.   move irrelevant objects from $\mathcal{C}$ to $\mathcal{R}$
10.   **endfor**
11.   **while** more split-points are available **do**
12.   check next time split point t_x (intersection)
13.   **if** $(u \in \mathcal{K})$ **and** $(v \in \mathcal{K})$ **then**
14.   update *CNN-list*
15.   exchange positions in k-list
16.   **endif**
17.   **if** $(u \in \mathcal{K})$ **and** $(v \in \mathcal{C})$ **then**
18.   move u from $\mathcal{K}$ to $\mathcal{C}$
19.   move v from $\mathcal{C}$ to $\mathcal{K}$
20.   update k-list
21.   update *CNN-list*
22.   **if** (v participates for the first time in k-list) **then**
23.   determine intersections of v with objects in $\mathcal{C}$
24.   update *split-list*
25.   **endif**
26.   **endif**
27.   **if** $(u \in \mathcal{C})$ **and** $(v \in \mathcal{C})$ **then**
28.   ignore split point t_x
29.   **endif**
30.   **endwhile**
31.   **return** *CNN-list, split-list*

Figure 5.6. The NNS-a algorithm.

Each object $o \in \mathcal{K}$ is responsible for a number of potential time split points, which are defined by the intersections of o and the objects contained in $\mathcal{C}$.

Therefore, each time an object is inserted into $\mathcal{K}$ intersection checks must be performed with the objects in $\mathcal{C}$. In order to reduce the number of intersection tests, if an object was previously inserted into $\mathcal{K}$ and now it is reinserted, it is not necessary to recompute the intersections. Moreover, according to Proposition 5.3, intersections at time points prior to the currently examined split point can be safely ignored.

Proposition 5.3
If there is a split point at time t_x, where $o_1 \in \mathcal{K}$ and $o_2 \in \mathcal{C}$ intersect, all intersections of o_2 with the other objects in $\mathcal{K}$ that occur at a time before t_x are not considered as split points.

Proof
This is evident, since the nearest neighbors of the query object up to time t_x have been already determined and therefore the intersections at time points prior to t_x do not denote a change in the result. $\square$

Evidently, to determine if two objects u and v intersect at some time point between t_s and t_e, we have to solve an equation. Let the square of the distance between P and the objects be described by the functions

$$D_{u,q}(t)^2 = u_1 \cdot t^2 + u_2 \cdot t + u_3$$

and

$$D_{v,q}(t)^2 = v_1 \cdot t^2 + v_2 \cdot t + v_3$$

respectively. In order for the two object to have an intersection in $[t_s, t_e]$ there must be at least one value t_x, where $t_s \leq t_x \leq t_e$ such that:

$$(u_1 - v_1) \cdot t_x^2 + (u_2 - v_2) \cdot t_x + (u_3 - v_3) = 0$$

From elementary calculus it is known that this equation can be satisfied by none, one, or two values of t_x. If

$$(u_2 - v_2)^2 - 4 \cdot (u_1 - v_1) \cdot (u_3 - v_3) < 0$$

then there is no intersection between u and v. If

$$(u_2 - v_2)^2 - 4 \cdot (u_1 - v_1) \cdot (u_3 - v_3) = 0$$

then the two objects intersect at

$$t_x = \frac{-(u_2 - v_2)}{2 \cdot (u_1 - v_1)}$$

Otherwise the objects intersect at two points t_x and t_y given by:

$$t_x = \frac{-(u_2 - v_2) + \sqrt{(u_2 - v_2)^2 - 4 \cdot (u_1 - v_1) \cdot (u_3 - v_3)}}{2 \cdot (u_1 - v_1)}$$

$$t_y = \frac{-(u_2 - v_2) - \sqrt{(u_2 - v_2)^2 - 4 \cdot (u_1 - v_1) \cdot (u_3 - v_3)}}{2 \cdot (u_1 - v_1)}$$

3.1.2 Algorithm NNS-b

After the execution of *NNS-a*, the *CNN-list* is formulated, which contains elements of the form $([t_1, t_2], o_1, o_2, ..., o_k)$, where $o_1, ..., o_k$ are the nearest neighbors of P from t_1 to t_2, in increasing distance order. Let S be the set containing the nearest neighbors of P at any given time between t_s and t_e. Clearly, $k \leq |S| \leq |\mathcal{O}|$. Assume now that we have to consider another object w, which was not known during the execution of *NNS-a*. We distinguish among the following cases, which describe the relation of w to the current answer:

case 1: w does not intersect any of the objects in S between t_s and t_e, and lies "above" the area of relevance. In this case, w is ignored, since it can not contribute to the nearest neighbors. The number of split points remains the same.

case 2: w does not intersect any of the objects in S between t_s and t_e, and lies completely "inside" the area of relevance. In this case w must be taken into account, since it affects the answer from t_s to t_e (Proposition 5.4). The number of split points may be reduced.

case 3: w intersects at least one object $v \in S$ at time $t_s \leq t_x \leq t_e$, but at time t_x v is not contained in the set of nearest neighbors. In this case, again w is ignored, since this intersection can not be considered as a split point because the answer is not affected. Therefore, no new split points are generated.

case 4: w intersects at least one object $v \in S$ at time $t_s \leq t_x \leq t_e$, and object v is contained in the set of nearest neighbors at time t_x. In this case w must be considered because at least one new split point is generated. We note, however, that some of the old split points may be discarded.

Proposition 5.4
Assume that a new object w does not intersect any of the nearest neighbors from t_s to t_e. If at time t_s its position among the k nearest neighbors is pos_w, then it maintains this position throughout the query duration.

Proof
Assume that there is a change in the result at some point t_x, where object w

changes its position among the nearest neighbors. This implies that there is an intersection at time t_x, since only an intersection denotes a result change. This contradicts our assumption that there are no intersections of w with other objects in the result. □

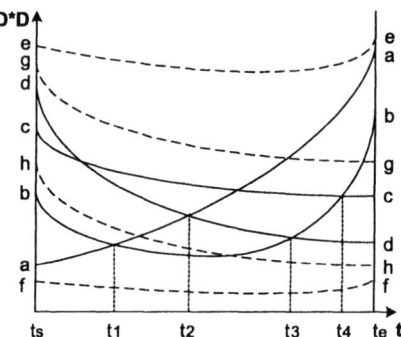

Figure 5.7. The four different cases that show the relation of a new object to the current nearest neighbors.

The aforementioned cases are depicted in Figure 5.7. Object e corresponds to *case 1*, since it is above the area of interest. Object f corresponds to *case 2*, because it is completely covered by the relevant area. Object g although intersects some objects, the time of these intersections are irrelevant to the answer, and therefore the situation corresponds to *case 3*. Finally, object h intersects a number of objects at time points that are critical to the answer and therefore corresponds to *case 4*.

The outline of the *NNS-b* algorithm is presented in Figure 5.8. Note that in lines 14 and 20 a call to the procedure *modify-CNN-list* is performed. This procedure, takes into consideration the *CNN-list* and the new *split-list* that is generated. It scans the *split-list* in increasing time order and performs the necessary modifications to the *CNN-list* and the *split-list*. Some split-points may be discarded during the process. The procedure steps are illustrated in Figure 5.9.

3.2 Query Processing with TPR-trees

Having described in detail the query processing algorithms in the previous section we are ready now to elaborate in the way these methods are combined with the TPR-tree. Let T be a TPR-tree which is built to index the underlying data. Starting from the root node of T the tree is searched in a depth-first-search manner (DFS). However, the proposed methods can also be combined with a breadth-first-search based algorithm. The first phase of the algorithm is com-

Nearest Neighbor Queries in Moving Objects

Algorithm *NNS-b*
Input: a list of elements of the form $([t_1, t_2], o_1, o_2, ..., o_k)$
where $o_1, ..., o_k$ are the NNs of P from t_1 to t_2 (*CNN list*),
a new object w, the *split-list*
Output: an updated list of the form $([t_1, t_2], o_1, o_2, ..., o_k)$
where $o_1, ..., o_k$ are the NNs of P from t_1 to t_2 (*CNN list*)
Local: k-list current list of NNs,
split-list, the current list of split points
1.   initialize S = union of NNs from t_s to t_e
2.   intersectionFlag = FALSE
3.   **foreach** $s \in S$ **do**
4.   check intersection between s and w
5.   **if** (s and w intersect) **then** // handle cases 3 and 4
6.   intersectionFlag = TRUE
7.   collect all t_j, s // t_j is where w and s intersect
8.   **if** (at t_j object s contributes to the NNs) **then**
9.   *update split-list*
10.   **endif**
11.   **endif**
12.   **endfor**
13.   **if** (intersectionFlag == TRUE) **then**
14.   call *modify-CNN-list*
15.   **else** // handle cases 1 and 2
16.   calculate $D_{q,w}(t)^2$ at time point t_s
17.   **if** $(D_{q,w}(t_s)^2 \geq D_{kNN}^2)$ **then**
18.   ignore w
19.   **else**
20.   call *modify-CNN-list*
21.   **endif**
22.   **endif**
23.   **return** *CNN-list*, *split-list*

Figure 5.8. The NNS-b algorithm.

pleted when $m \geq k$ objects have been collected from the dataset. Tree branches are selected to descent according to the $MINDIST$ metric [106] (Definition 1) between the moving query and bounding rectangles at time t_s. These m moving objects are used as input to the *NNS-a* algorithm to determine the result from t_s to t_e. Therefore, up to now we have a first version of the *split-list* and the *CNN-list*. However, other relevant objects may reside in leaf nodes of T that are not yet examined.

Definition 5.1
Given a point p at $(p_1, p_2, ..., p_n)$ and a rectangle r whose lower-left and upper-right corners are $(s_1, s_2, ..., s_n)$ and $(t_1, t_2, ..., t_n)$, the distance $MINDIST(p, r)$

Procedure *modify-CNN-list*
Input: a list of elements $([t_1, t_2], o_1, o_2, ..., o_k)$
where $o_1, ..., o_k$ are the NNs of P from t_1 to t_2 (CNN list),
a new object w, the *split-list*
Output: an updated list of elements $([t_1, t_2], o_1, o_2, ..., o_k)$
where $o_1, ..., o_k$ are the NNs of P from t_1 to t_2 (CNN list)
Local: k-list current list of NNs
1.   calculate $D_{q,w}(t)^2$ at time point t_s
2.   consult *CNN-list* and update the current k-list
3.   **while** more split-points are available **do**
4.   check next split-point $(t_x, \{u, v\})$
5.   update *CNN-list*
6.   **if** $(u \notin k - list)$ **and** $(v \notin k - list)$ **then**
7.   remove split-point $(t_x, \{u, v\})$
8.   **elseif** $(u \in k - list)$ **and** $(v \notin k - list)$ **then**
9.   remove u from k-list
10.   insert v in k-list
11.   update k-list
12.   **elseif** $(v \in k - list)$ **and** $(u \notin k - list)$ **then**
13.   remove v from k-list
14.   insert u in k-list
15.   update k-list
16.   **else**
17.   exchange positions between u **and** v
18.   update k-list
19.   **endif**
20.   **endwhile**

Figure 5.9. The modify-CNN-list procedure.

is defined as follows:

$$MINDIST(p, r) = \sqrt{\sum_{j=1}^{n} |p_j - r_j|^2}$$

where:

$$r_j = \begin{cases} s_j, & p_j < s_j \\ t_j, & p_j > t_j \\ p_j, & \text{otherwise} \end{cases}$$

$\square$

In the second phase of the algorithm, the DFS continues searching the tree, by selecting **possibly relevant tree branches** and discarding non-relevant ones. Every time a **possibly relevant moving object** is reached, algorithm *NNS-b* is called to update the *split-list* and the *CNN-list* of the result. The algorithm terminates when there are no relevant branches to examine.

Nearest Neighbor Queries in Moving Objects

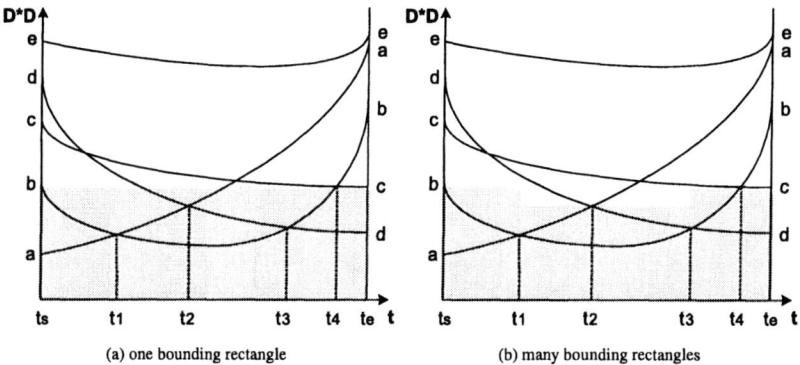

Figure 5.10. Pruning techniques.

In order to complete the algorithm description, the terms **possibly relevant tree branches** and **possibly relevant moving objects** must be clarified. In other words, the pruning strategy must be described in detail. Figure 5.10 illustrates two possible pruning techniques that can be used to determine relevant and non-relevant tree branches and moving objects:

Pruning Technique 1 (PT1): According to this technique we keep track of the maximum distance $MAXDIST$ between the query and the current set of nearest neighbors. In Figure 5.10(a) this distance is defined between the query and object b at time t_{start}. We formulate a **moving bounding rectangle** R centered at P with extends $MAXDIST$ in each dimension and moving with the same velocity vector as P. If R intersects a bounding rectangle E in an internal node, the corresponding tree branch may contain objects that contribute to the answer and therefore must be examined further. Otherwise, it can be safely rejected since it is impossible to contain relevant objects. In the same manner, if a moving object o_x found in a leaf node intersects R it may contribute to the answer, otherwise it is rejected.

Pruning Technique 2 (PT2): This technique differs from the previous one with respect to the granularity level, where moving bounding rectangles are formulated. Instead of using only one bounding rectangle, a set of bounding rectangles is defined according to the currently determined split points. Note that it is not necessary to consider all split points, but only these that are defined by the k-th nearest neighbor in each time interval. An example set of moving bounding rectangles is illustrated in Figure 5.10(b). Each internal bounding rectangle and moving object is checked for intersection against the whole set of moving bounding rectangles and it is considered relevant only if it intersects at least one of them.

Other pruning techniques can also be determined by grouping split points to keep the balance between the number of generated bounding rectangles and the existing empty space. Several pruning techniques can be combined in a single search by selecting the preferred technique according to some criteria (e.g., current number of split-points, existing empty space).

It is anticipated that PT1 will be more efficient with respect to CPU time, but less efficient concerning I/O time, because the **empty space** will cause unnecessary disk accesses. On the other hand, PT2 seems to incur more CPU overhead due to the increased number of intersection computations, but also less I/O time owing to the detailed pruning performed. Based on the above discussion, we define the *NNS-CON* algorithm which operates on TPR-trees and can be used with either of the two pruning techniques. The algorithm outline is illustrated in In Figure 5.11.

Algorithm *NNS-CON*
Input: the TPR-tree root,
   a moving query P,
   the number k of NNs
Output: the k NNs in $[t_s, t_e]$
Local: a set $\mathcal{O}$ of collected objects,
   $Flag$ is FALSE if *NNS-a* has not yet been called
number col of collected objects
1. **if** ($node$ is LEAF) **then**
2.   **if** ($|\mathcal{O}| < k$) **then**
3.   add each entry of $node$ to $\mathcal{O}$
4.   update $|\mathcal{O}|$
5.   **endif**
6.   **if** ($|\mathcal{O}| \geq k$) **and** ($Flag$ == FALSE) **then**
7.   call *NNS-a*
8.   set Flag=TRUE
9.   **elseif** ($|\mathcal{O}| \geq k$) **and** ($Flag$ == TRUE) **then**
10.   apply pruning technique
11.   for each entry of $node$ call *NNS-b*
12.   **endif**
13. **elseif** ($node$ is INTERNAL) **then**
14.   apply pruning technique
15.   sort entries of $node$ wrt $MINDIST$ at t_s
16.   call *NNS-CON* recursively
17. **endif**

Figure 5.11. The NNS-CON algorithm.

4. Performance Evaluation
4.1 Preliminaries

In the sequel, a description of the performance evaluation procedure is given, aiming at providing a comparison study among the different processing methods. The methods under consideration are: i) the *NNS-CON* algorithm enabled by *Pruning Technique 1* described in the previous section, and ii) the *NNS-REP* algorithm which operates by posing repetitive NN queries to the TPR-tree [130]. Both algorithms as well as the TPR-tree access method have been implemented in the C programming language.

Parameter	Value
database size, N	10K, 50K, 100K, 1M
space dimensions, d	1, 2, 3
data distribution, D	uniform, gaussian
number of NNs, k	1 - 100
travel time, t_{travel}	26 - 1048 sec.
LRU buffer size, B	0.1% - 20% of tree pages

Table 5.2. Parameters and corresponding values.

There are several parameters that contribute to the method performance. These parameters, along with their respective values assigned during the experimentation are summarized in Table 5.2.

The datasets used for the experimentation are synthetically generated using the uniform or the gauss distribution. The dataspace extends are 1,000,000 × 1,000,000 meters and the velocity vectors of the moving objects are uniformly generated, with speed values between 0 and 30 m/sec. Based on these objects, a TPR-tree is constructed. The TPR-tree page size is fixed at 2Kbytes.

The query workload is composed of 500 uniformly distributed queries having the same characteristics (length, velocity). The comparison study is performed by using several performance metrics, such as: i) the number of disk accesses, ii) the CPU-time, iii) the I/O time and iv) the total running time. In order to accurately estimate the I/O time for each method a disk model is used to model the disk, instead of assigning a constant value for each disk access [108]. Since the usage of a buffer plays a very important role for the query performance we assume the existence of an LRU buffer with size varying between 0.1% and 20% of the database size.

The results presented here correspond to uniformly distributed datasets. Results performed for gaussian distributions of data and queries demonstrated similar performance and therefore are omitted. The main difference between the two distributions is that in the case of the gaussian distribution, the algorithms require more resources since the data density increases and therefore more split-points and distance computations are needed to evaluate the queries.

4.2 Experimental Results

Several experimental series have been conducted to test the performance of the different methods. The experimental series are summarized in Table 5.3.

Experiment	Varying Parameter	Fixed Parameters
EXP1	NNs, k	$N = 1M$, $B = 10\%$, $t_{travel} = 110$ sec. $d = 2$, D=uniform
EXP2	buffer size, B	$N = 1M$, $k = 5$, $t_{travel} = 110$ sec. $d = 2$, D=uniform
EXP3	travel time, t_{travel}	$N = 1M$, $k = 5$, $B = 10\%$, $d = 2$, D=uniform
EXP4	space dimensions, d NNs, k	$N = 1M$, $B = 10\%$, $t_{travel} = 110$ sec. D=uniform
EXP5	database size, N NNs, k	$B = 500$ pages, $d = 2$, D=uniform, $t_{travel} = 110$ sec.

Table 5.3. Experiments conducted.

The purpose of the first experiment (EXP1) is to investigate the behavior of the methods for various values of the requested nearest neighbors. The corresponding results are depicted in Figure 5.12. By increasing k, more split points are introduced for the *NNS-CON* method, whereas more influence calculations are needed by the *NNS-REP* method. It is evident that *NNS-CON* outperforms significantly the *NNS-REP* method. Although both methods are highly affected by k, the performance of *NNS-REP* degrades more rapidly. As Figure 5.12(a) illustrates, *NNS-REP* requires a large number of node accesses. However, since there is a high locality in the page references performed by a query, the page faults are limited. As a result, the performance difference occurs due to the increased CPU cost required by *NNS-REP* (Figure 5.13). Another interesting observation derived from Figure 5.13 is that the CPU cost becomes more significant than the I/O cost by increasing the number of nearest neighbors.

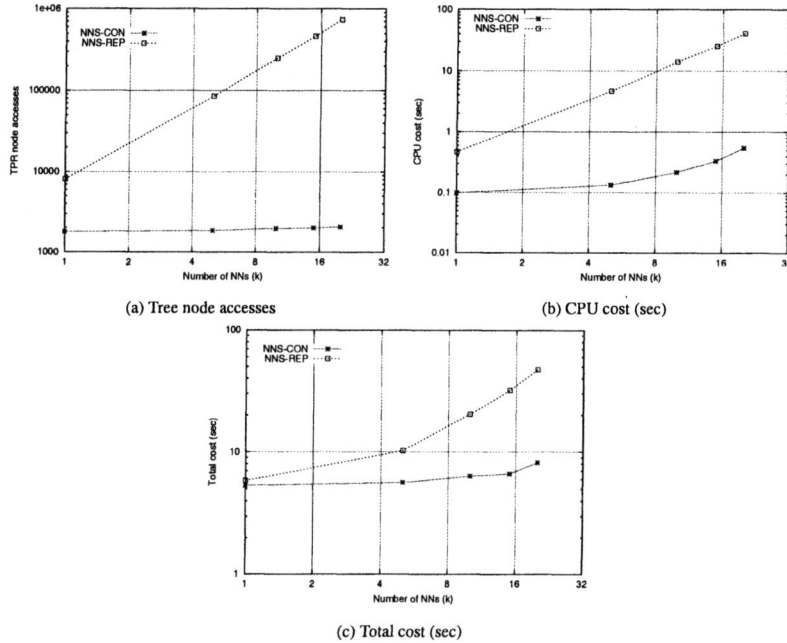

Figure 5.12. Results for different values of the number of nearest neighbors.

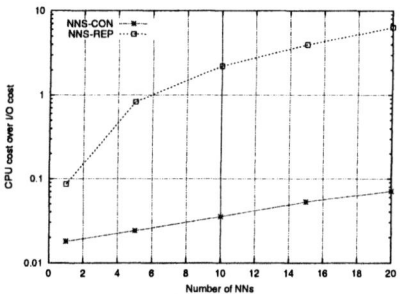

Figure 5.13. CPU cost over I/O cost.

The next experiment (EXP2) illustrates the impact of the buffer capacity (Figure 5.14). Evidently, the more buffer space is available the less disk accesses are required by both methods. It is interesting that although the number of node accesses required by *NNS-REP* is very large, (see Figure 5.12(a)) the buffer manages to reduce the number of disk accesses significantly due to buffer hits. However, even if the buffer capacity is limited, *NNS-CON* demonstrates excellent performance.

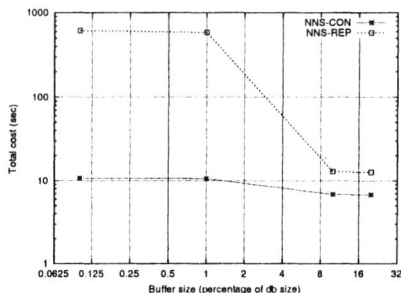

Figure 5.14. Results for different buffer capacities.

Experiment EXP3 demonstrates the impact of the travel time on the performance of the methods. The corresponding results are depicted in Figure 5.15. Small travel times are favorable for both methods, because less CPU and I/O operations are required. On the other hand, large travel times increase the number of split-points and the number of distance computations, since the probability that there is a change in the result increases. However, *NNS-CON* performs much better for large travel times in contrast to *NNS-REP* whose performance is affected significantly.

The next experiment (EXP4) demonstrates the impact of the space dimensionality. The increase in the dimensionality has the following results: i) the database size increases due to smaller tree fanout, ii) the TPR-tree quality degrades due to overlap increase in bounding rectangles of internal nodes, and iii) the CPU cost increases because more computations are required for distance calculations. Both methods are affected by the dimensionality increase. However, by observing the relative performance of the methods (*NNS-REP* over *NNS-CON*) in 2-d and 3-d space illustrated in Figure 5.16, it is realized that *NNS-REP* is affected more significantly by the number of space dimensions.

Finally, Figure 5.17 depicts the impact of database size (EXP5). In this experiment, the buffer capacity is fixed at 500 pages, and the number of moving objects is set between 10,000 and 100,000. The number of requested nearest neighbors is varying between 1 and 15, whereas the travel time is fixed at 110 sec. By increasing the number of moving objects, more tree nodes are generated and, therefore, more time is needed to search the TPR-tree. Moreover, by keeping the buffer capacity constant, the buffer hit ratio decreases, producing

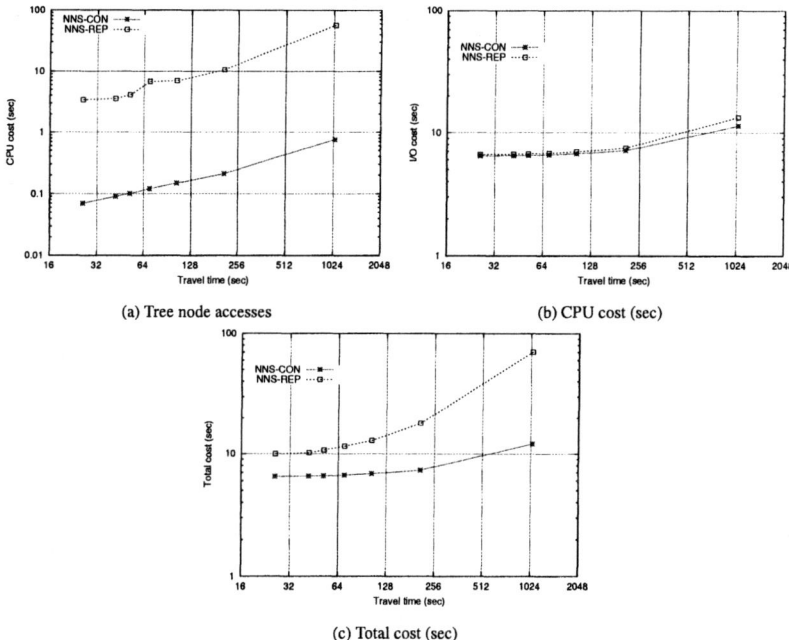

Figure 5.15. Results for different values of the travel time.

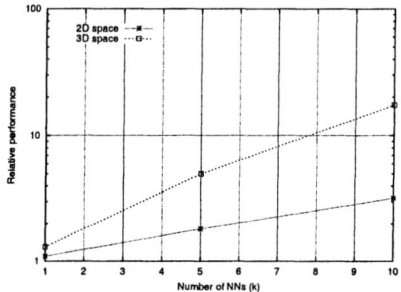

Figure 5.16. Results for different space dimensions.

more page faults. As Figure 5.17 illustrates, the performance ratio (*NNS-REP* over *NNS-CON*) increases with the database size.

5. Summary

Applications that rely on the combination of spatial and temporal object characteristics demand new types of queries and efficient query processing

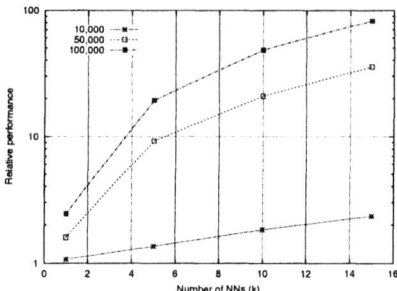

Figure 5.17. Results for different database size.

techniques. An important query type in such a case is the k nearest neighbor query, which requires the determination of the k closest objects to the query for a given time interval $[t_s, t_e]$. The major difficulty in such a case is that both queries and objects change positions continuously, and therefore the methods that solve the problem for the static case can not be applied directly.

In this chapter, we performed a study of efficient methods for NN query processing in moving-object databases, and several performance evaluation experiments to compare their efficiency. The main conclusion is that the proposed algorithm outperforms significantly the repetitive approach for different parameter values. Future research may focus on:

- extending the algorithm to work with moving rectangles (although the extension is simple, the algorithmic complexity increases due to more distance computations),

- providing cost estimates concerning the number of node accesses, the number of intersection checks and the number of distance computations, and

- adapting the method to operate on access methods which store past positions of objects (trajectories) to answer past queries.

6. Further Reading

Many research efforts have focused on indexing schemes and efficient processing techniques for moving-object datasets [4, 37, 54, 110, 124, 136]. Indexing and query processing for past positions of objects are addressed in many research works such as [66, 81, 100, 129, 146]. Indexing issues for present and future positions of objects are addressed in [4, 44, 47, 53, 54, 60, 77, 110, 144].

Recently, there is an interest in indexing and query processing for moving objects whose movement is constraint by an underlying spatial network (e.g., a road network, a railway network). Some important research results in the issue have been reported in [91, 117, 120].

III

NEAREST NEIGHBOR SEARCH WITH MULTIPLE RESOURCES

Chapter 6

PARALLEL AND DISTRIBUTED DATABASES

1. Introduction

One of the primary goals in database research is the investigation of innovative techniques in order to provide more efficient query processing. This goal becomes much more important considering that modern applications are more resource demanding, and are usually based on multiuser systems. A database research direction that has been widely accepted by developers is the exploitation of multiple resources (e.g., processors, disks) towards more efficient processing.

The exploitation of multiple computer resources can be performed by using either a *parallel database system* or a *distributed database system*. Although there are several similarities between these two approaches, there are also some fundamental differences. Examples of the two approaches are given in Figure 6.1.

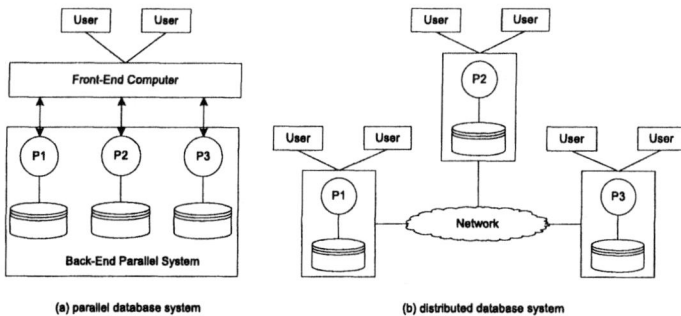

Figure 6.1. Parallel and distributed database systems.

In a parallel database system, usually the processors are *tightly coupled* in a single computer system. However, in some cases (e.g., networks of workstations) processors are loosely coupled and reside in different machines. Processors cooperate to provide efficient query processing. The user is not aware of the parallelism, since she has no access to a specific processor of the system. According to the parallel architecture, the processors may have access to a common memory, or they can communicate by message passing. In the latter case the processor interconnection is achieved by means of high-speed links. Parallelism can be categorized in:

- *CPU parallelism*: A task is partitioned to several processors for execution

- *I/O parallelism*: The data are partitioned to several secondary storage units (disks or CD-ROMs) to achieve better I/O performance.

Distributed database systems are usually *loosely coupled* and are composed by independent machines. Moreover, each machine is capable of running its own applications and serve its own users. Data are partitioned to the different machines, and therefore several machines should be accessed to answer a user query. Due to the loosely coupled approach, the network communication cost is significant and should be taken into consideration. Specialized algorithms for distributed query processing, distributed query optimization and distributed transaction support have been proposed to provide efficient access to physically distributed data. As in the case of parallel database systems, a distributed database system should provide *distribution transparency*. In other words, users and applications need not worry about the data distribution. The distributed DBMS is responsible to deliver the appropriate data from remote hosts.

2. Multidisk Systems

Generally, in a database system the data collection resides on disk unit(s). In addition, the index that is used to provide access to the data is also stored on disk. In some cases the index size is small enough to be maintained in main-memory. However, a database system usually manages more than one indexes and therefore it is not possible to keep all of them in-core. Since generally an index is stored on disk, one of the I/O technologies that have affected access method design is the disk array. A disk array is composed of two or more disks, each one containing different database parts.

Using more than one disk devices leads to increased system throughput, since the workload is balanced among the participating disks and many operations can be processed in parallel. RAID systems have been introduced in [99] as an inexpensive solution to the I/O bottleneck. Using more than one disk devices, leads to increased system throughput, since the workload is balanced among the participating disks and many operations can be processed in parallel [19, 20].

A typical layout of a disk array architecture is illustrated in Figure 6.2, where four disks are attached to a processor.

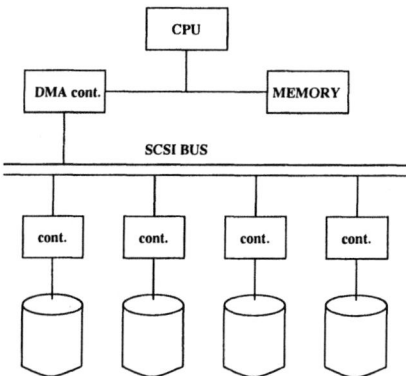

Figure 6.2. Example of disk array architecture.

Given a multidisk architecture, one faces the problem of partitioning the data and the associated access information to take advantage of the I/O parallelism. The way data are partitioned reflects the performance of read/write operations. The declustering problem attracted many researchers and a lot of work has been performed towards taking advantage of the I/O parallelism, to support data intensive applications. Techniques for B^+-tree declustering have been reported in [113]. In [149] the authors study effective declustering schemes for the grid file structure, whereas parallel M-trees are studied in [147]. Here we focus on the R-tree access method. The challenge is to decluster an R-tree structure among the available disks to:

1 distribute the workload during query processing as evenly as possible among the disks, and

2 activate as few disks as possible.

There are several alternative designs that could be followed to take advantage of the multiple disk architecture. These alternatives have been studied in [48], and are briefly discussed below:

Independent R-trees
The data are partitioned among the available disks, and an R-tree is build for each disk (see Figure 6.3). The performance depends on how the data distribution is performed:

- *data distribution*: The data objects are assigned to different disks in a *round-robin* manner, or by using a hash function. This method guarantees that each disk will host approximately the same number of objects. However, even for small queries, all disks are likely to be activated to answer the query.

- *space distribution*: The space is divided to d partitions, where d is the number of available disks. The drawback of this approach is that due to the non-uniformity of real-life datasets, some disks may host a greater number of objects than other disks, and therefore may become a bottleneck. Moreover, for large queries (large query regions) this method fails to balance the load equally among all disks.

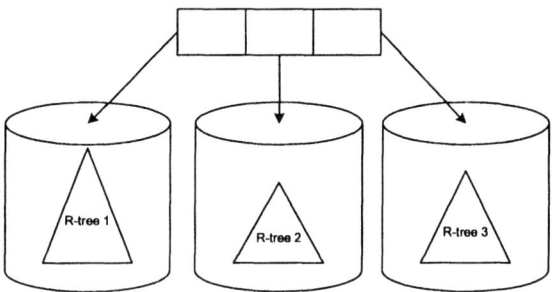

Figure 6.3. Independent R-trees.

R-tree with Super Nodes

This alternative uses only one R-tree (see Figure 6.4). The exploitation of the multiple disks is obtained by expanding each tree node. More specifically, the logical size of the tree node becomes d times larger, and therefore each node is partitioned to all d disks (disk stripping). Although the load is equally balanced during query processing, all disks are activated in each query. This happens because since there is no total order of the rectangles (MBRs) that are hosted in a tree node, each node must be reconstructed by accessing all the disks (each

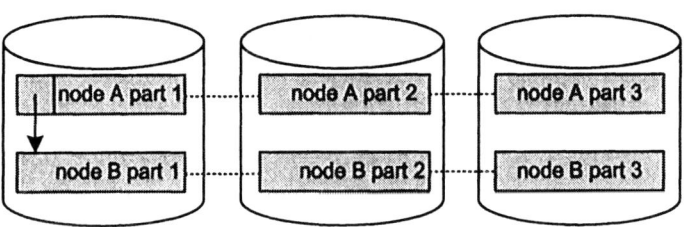

Figure 6.4. R-tree with super-nodes.

node is partitioned among all disks).

Multiplexed (MX) R-tree

This alternative uses a single R-tree, having its nodes distributed among the disks. The main difference with an ordinary R-tree is that interdisk pointers are used to formulate the tree structure. Each node pointer is a pair of the form $<diskID, pageID>$, where $diskID$ is the disk identifier containing the page $pageID$. An example MX R-tree with 13 nodes distributed in 3 disks is given in Figure 6.5. The number near each node denotes the disk where the node resides.

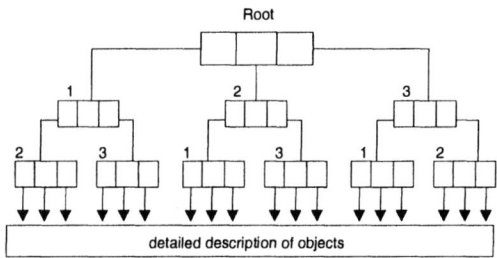

Figure 6.5. MX R-tree example.

The main issue that must be explained is the node-to-disk assignment policy. The insertion of new objects will cause some nodes to split. The problem is to which disk the newly created node N_n will be assigned, and the target is to minimize the query response time. In order to obtain the best result, we could examine all nodes that lie in the same tree level. However, this operation is very costly because it results in many I/O operations. Instead, only the sibling nodes are examined, i.e. the nodes that have the same parent with N_n. Moreover, it is not necessary to fetch the sibling nodes, since the information that we require (MBRs) resides in the parent node (which has been fetched already in memory to insert the new object). There are several criteria that could be used to perform the placement of the new node N_n:

- *data balance*: In the best case, all disks must host the same number of tree nodes. If a disk contains more nodes than the others, it may become a bottleneck during query processing.

- *area balance*: The area that each disk covers plays a very important role when we answer range queries. A disk that covers a large area, will be accessed with higher probability than the others, and therefore it may become a bottleneck.

- *proximity*: If two nodes are near in space, the probability that they will be accessed together is high. Therefore, proximal nodes should be stored to different disks to maximize parallelism.

Although it is very difficult to satisfy all criteria simultaneously, some heuristics have been proposed to attack the problem:

- *round-robin*: The new node is assigned to a disk using the round-robin algorithm.
- *minimum area*: This heuristic assigns the new node to the disk that covers the smallest area.
- *minimum intersection*: This heuristic assigns the new node to a disk trying to minimize the overlap between the new node and the nodes that are already stored in this disk.
- *proximity index*: This heuristic is based on the proximity measure which compares two rectangles and calculates the probability that they will be accessed together by the same query. Therefore, rectangles (which correspond to tree nodes) with high proximity must be stored in different disks.

Several experimental results have been reported in [48]. The main conclusion is that the MXR-tree with the proximity index method for node-to-disk assignment outperforms the other methods. The performance evaluation has been conducted by using uniformly distributed spatial objects and uniformly distributed range queries. The proposed method manages to activate few disks for small range queries, and activate all disks for large queries, achieving good load balancing, and therefore can be used as an efficient method for parallelizing the R-tree structure. It would be interesting to investigate the performance of the method for non-uniform distributions.

The MXR-tree access method is used in Chapter 7 to support NN query processing in a multidisk system. The branch-and-bound nature of the fundamental NN algorithm leads to decreased parallelism exploitation. Therefore, new algorithms are required that could take advantage of the multiple disk units in a more efficient way.

3. Multiprocessor Systems

The design of algorithms for multiple resource exploitation is not a trivial task. Although in some cases the parallel version of a serial algorithm is straightforward, one must look carefully at three fundamental performance measures:

1 *speed-up*: The speed-up measure shows the capability of the algorithm when the number of processors is increased and the input size is constant.

Parallel and Distributed Databases

The perfect speed-up is the linear speed-up, meaning that if T seconds are required to perform the operation with one processor, then $T/2$ seconds are required to perform the same operation using two processors.

2 *size-up*: Size-up shows the behavior of the algorithm when the input size is increased and the number of processors remains constant.

3 *scale-up*: Finally, scale-up shows the performance of the algorithm when both the input size and the number of processors are increased.

There are three basic parallel architectures that have been used in research and development fields (see Figure 6.6):

- *shared everything*: All processors share the same resources (memory and disks), whereas the communication among processors is performed by means of the global memory.

- *shared disk*: All processors share the disks but each one has its own memory.

- *shared nothing*: The processors use different disks and different memory units, whereas the communication among processors is performed using message passing mechanisms.

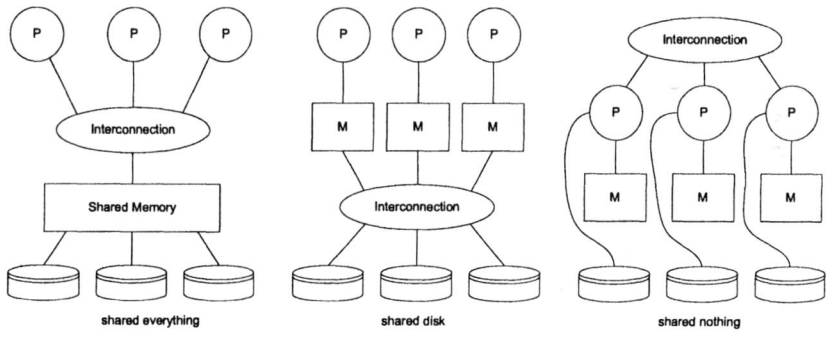

Figure 6.6. Parallel architectures.

As in a multidisk system, in a multiprocessor system several issues must be taken into consideration to guarantee acceptable performance. In the sequel, we focus on the shared-nothing architecture, which is the most promising with respect to scalability [26]. Since each processor controls its own disk unit(s) we are facing (again) the problem of data distribution. Moreover, interprocessor communication costs must be considered, since in many cases this cost is significant and affects query processing performance. Apart from data distribution, index distribution is another important issue.

In [58] Koudas et. al. propose an R-tree distribution technique to support spatial range queries in a *network of workstations*. However, this technique can be applied to any shared-nothing parallel architecture as well. The R-tree leaf level is distributed to the available computers, whereas the upper tree levels are stored in the master. Since, the upper R-tree levels occupy relatively little space, they can be kept in main memory. Given that the dataset is known in advance, Koudas et. al. suggest sorting the data with respect to the Hilbert values of the MBRs' centroid. Then, the tree leaf level is formed, and the assignment of leaves to sites is performed in a round-robin manner. This method guarantees that leaves that contain objects close in the address space will be assigned to different sites, thus increasing the parallelism during range query processing. In Figure 6.8 we present a way to decluster the R-tree of Figure 6.7 in three sites, one primary and two secondary.

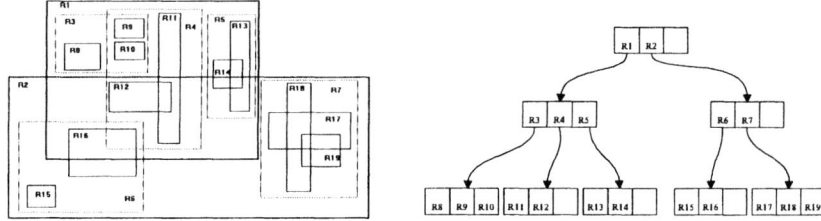

Figure 6.7. R-tree example.

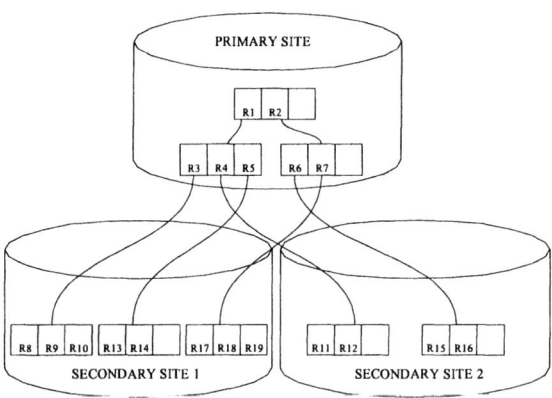

Figure 6.8. Declustering an R-tree over three sites.

This architecture is used in Chapter 8 to process NN queries. Although the fundamental NN algorithm for R-trees is directly applicable, its performance

Parallel and Distributed Databases 83

is not expected to be satisfactory due to increased communication costs posed by its branch-and-bound nature. Therefore, we provide efficient algorithms that are more appropriate in a parallel setting, by accessing several processors concurrently.

4. Distributed Systems

A distributed database is supported by a number of computers that are loosely coupled, and communicate by means of a network configuration. Communication costs are even more important than in a shared-nothing parallel architecture. In such a configuration, each computer may run its own applications and participate in query processing if this is necessary. Data are partitioned and according to access patterns may be replicated as well, to increase query processing performance and avoid communication costs when needed. For example, in a distributed database system based on the relational data model, a relation (table) may be *fragmented* horizontally (row-wise) or vertically (column-wise). The various *fragments* are distributed to the available computer systems, by allowing storing the same fragment to more than one computers. An example of horizontal and vertical fragmentation is depicted in Figure 6.9.

ID	Name	Population	Country	X	Y	
1	Athens	4,000,000	Greece	700	100	} Computer 1
2	Vienna	1,850,000	Austria	350	500	
3	Amsterdam	2,100,000	Netherlands	600	600	} Computer 2
4	Madrid	5,150,000	Spain	200	200	
5	Rome	3,300,000	Italy	350	400	} Computer 3
6	Paris	9,800,000	France	300	600	

(a) horizontal fragmentation

ID	Name	Population		ID	Country		ID	X	Y
1	Athens	4,000,000		1	Greece		1	700	100
2	Vienna	1,850,000		2	Austria		2	350	500
3	Amsterdam	2,100,000		3	Netherlands		3	600	600
4	Madrid	5,150,000		4	Spain		4	200	200
5	Rome	3,300,000		5	Italy		5	350	400
6	Paris	9,800,000		6	France		6	300	600

　　　　Computer 1　　　　　　　　Computer 2　　　　　　　Computer 3
(b) vertical fragmentation

Figure 6.9. Horizontal and vertical fragmentation.

We assume that a spatial relation has been horizontally fragmented and distributed to a number of databases, which may be *heterogeneous* (i.e., they may be based on different data models and architectures). The system is composed of a primary server that operates as a coordinator for the source databases. All systems communicate via a network configuration (see Figure 6.10). We assume that query requests are initiated by a user's system and then submitted to the primary server for evaluation. Also, the query results are gathered from the source databases to the primary server and then are shipped back to the appropriate user's system. Despite the fact that we perform a distinction between primary and secondary sites, any secondary site could take responsibility of evaluating user queries. Each source database has complete control over the objects that it stores. Therefore, different access methods and optimization techniques may be utilized by different databases.

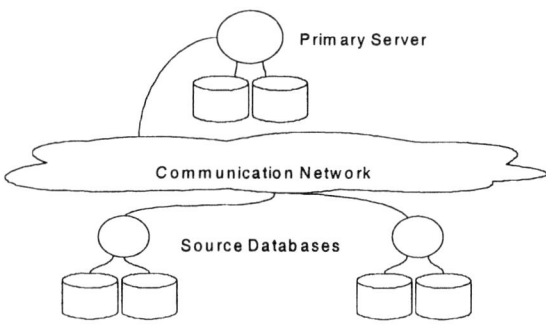

Figure 6.10. Distributed database architecture.

In such a system, the challenge is to support similarity queries, and particularly k-NN queries, as efficiently as possible. In Chapter 9 we study exactly this problem, where several different processing methods are proposed and evaluated experimentally. Answering similarity queries in a distributed system is considered very important, taking into consideration the exponential growth of the world wide web (WWW), where millions of computer systems are connected to form a large pool of useful information.

5. Summary

The exploitation of multiple system resources is considered a promising approach towards increased query processing efficiency. In this chapter we discussed briefly the basic concepts of parallel and distributed database systems. In order to take advantage of multiple resources (processors and disks) efficient data partitioning, index partitioning and query processing methods should be designed. In cases where the processors are loosely coupled, the communication cost must be taken into account, since it is quite significant, specifically for low-bandwidth network configurations.

We separate amongst three different configurations, namely: 1) multidisk systems, 2) multiprocessor systems and 3) distributed systems. For each case we briefly discussed the main arising issues. The three upcoming chapters deal with the above system architectures separately, with respect to NN query processing.

6. Further Reading

There is a significant amount of research work regarding parallel and distributed database systems. Two very important textbooks on distributed database systems are the books by Ceri and Pelagatti [18], and Ozsu and Valduriez [86]. Although a lot of research has been performed since the publishing time of these textbooks, the issues studied in [18, 86] are very important to understand the main ideas behind data distribution and distributed query processing.

A collection of important research papers for parallel relational database systems can be found in [67]. Some of the issues covered are: parallel database architectures, parallel sorting, parallel join processing and parallel query optimization.

Chapter 7

MULTIDISK QUERY PROCESSING

1. Introduction

Nowadays, several large databases world-wide are supported by large storage devices that are capable of servicing many I/O requests in parallel. This is feasible by exploiting disk array technology aiming at both increased data availability and increased I/O throughput. Data availability is increased because if a disk failure occurs, access to the corresponding data is provided by the other disk array units. Throughput increase is feasible, since two concurrent requests for the same data can be served (probably) by different disk units. However, throughput is highly dependent on the specific disk array architecture used, and the data striping method supported by the disk controller.

In the majority of cases, an algorithm suitable for a uni-disk system is not appropriate in a multidisk architecture. Therefore, existing uni-disk methods should be adapted accordingly to provide acceptable query processing performance, In this respect, this chapter studies the problem of NN query processing in a multidisk system. It is assumed that an R-tree is used to index the underlying dataset, which is composed of multidimensional points.

The material of this chapter is based on [95] and is organized as follows. In the next section we discuss several algorithms that could be used to process NN queries in a multidisk system. Among them, the NN algorithm studied in Chapter 3 is also briefly discussed for completeness. Two more algorithms are given, namely: the *full-parallel similarity search* and the *candidate reduction similarity search*. Moreover, a hypothetical optimal algorithm is given, which performs the minimum possible number of disk accesses, and it is used for comparison purposes. Section 3 contains the performance evaluation performed based on real-life and synthetic datasets. Finally, Section 4 summarizes the work.

2. Algorithms

In this section we discuss several algorithms for NN query processing in case of a multidisk system. We begin our exploration with the NN algorithm discussed in Chapter 3. Since this algorithm is based on branch-and-bound, it is not directly applicable in a parallel setting. Therefore two more algorithms are given that are more appropriate for a multidisk system. For comparison reasons, an hypothetical optimal algorithm is also given, which issues the minimum possible number of disk accesses.

2.1 The Branch-and-Bound Algorithm

The first algorithm is essentially the algorithm proposed by Roussopoulos et. al. [106]. This algorithm has been described in detail in Chapter 3. Here we only review some of the fundamental characteristics. The algorithm is based on a branch-and-bound R-tree search. In order to find the nearest neighbor of a query point, the algorithm starts form the R-tree root and proceeds towards the leaf level. The key idea of the algorithm is that many tree branches can be discarded according to some basic rules. These rules use two fundamental distances, $MINDIST(P, R)$ and $MINMAXDIST(P, R)$ between a rectangle R and a point P.

In order to process general k-NN queries, an ordered sequence of the current k most promising answers has to be maintained, and the MBR pruning has to be performed with respect to the furthest distance. Thus, an MBR R is discarded if $MINDIST(R, P)$ from the query point P is greater than the actual distance from the query point to its k-th nearest neighbor. Henceforth, this algorithm will be referred to as **B**ranch and **B**ound **S**imilarity **S**earch (**BBSS**).

2.2 Full-Parallel Similarity Search

An efficient algorithm for similarity search on disk arrays must be characterized by some fundamental properties:

- parallelism must be exploited as much as possible,
- the number of retrieved nodes must be minimized,
- the response time of user queries should be reduced as much as possible, and
- throughput must be maximized.

Usually, if the first three properties hold then the last also holds. The problem is that the first two properties are contradictory for similarity search.

Observing how the sequential algorithm works, we see that a careful refinement of the candidate nodes is performed, trying to avoid node accesses that will not contribute to the final answer. In order to exploit I/O parallelism in

Multidisk Query Processing 89

similarity search, we have to access several nodes (residing in different disks) in parallel. Intuitively this implies that the granularity of the refinement must be coarsened. This also implies that some of the accessed nodes eventually will be proved irrelevant with respect to the final answer, and therefore they should have never been accessed.

Compare the above scheme with a range query. A range query is described by a well-defined region of arbitrary shape (usually hyper-rectangular or hyper-spherical) and all objects intersecting this region are requested. After a node is accessed, we are able to determine which of its children need to be visited by inspecting the corresponding MBRs that are located in the node. Then, the disks that host the relevant children nodes can be activated in parallel. Evidently, the visiting sequence of the relevant nodes is not important, since any such sequence leads to the same answer (assuming only read-only operations). On the other hand, in similarity search, the visiting order is the most important parameter in performance efficiency, since it is responsible for the further pruning of irrelevant nodes. Note that even in range query processing, an accessed node may not contribute to the final answer, but this fact is due to empty space and the use of conservative approximations, and it is irrelevant to the visiting order of the nodes. Therefore, we come up with a problem definition, which is stated as follows:

Problem Definition
Given a query point P in n-d space and an integer number k, **determine** an efficient search of the parallel R*-tree, **in order to** report the k nearest neighbors of P, **trying to** (i) maximize parallelism, (ii) access as few nodes as possible, and (iii) reduce response time. □

From the above discussion we observe that two fundamental sub-problems must be solved:

- to determine an effective way of pruning irrelevant nodes in every tree level, and
- to use a clever criterion to decide which nodes and when are going to be accessed in parallel.

In the remaining of this subsection we develop a query processing technique aiming to solve the aforementioned problems and reach the targets presented in the beginning of this subsection. We continue with an important definition regarding the maximum possible distance $MAXDIST$ between a point and a hyper-rectangle.

Definition 7.1
The distance $MAXDIST$ between a query point P and an MBR R is the

distance from P to the furthest vertex of R and equals:

$$MAXDIST(P, R) = \sqrt{\sum_{j=1}^{n} |p_j - r_j|^2}$$

where:

$$r_j = \begin{cases} t_j, & p_j \leq \frac{s_j + t_j}{2} \\ s_j, & \text{otherwise} \end{cases}$$

□

To distinguish between the three distances ($MINDIST, MINMAXDIST$ and $MAXDIST$) an example is illustrated in Figure 7.1, showing a point, two rectangles and the corresponding distances.

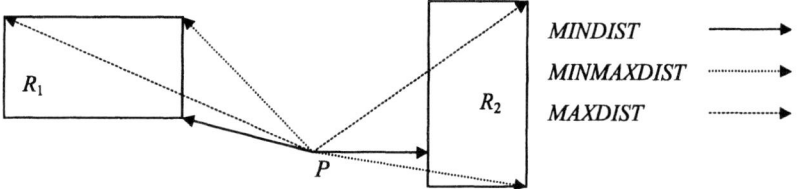

Figure 7.1. $MINDIST, MINMAXDIST$ and $MAXDIST$ between a point P and two rectangles R_1 and R_2.

We continue with a general description of a similarity search strategy in disk arrays. Later we investigate more thoroughly the important points and provide values for the parameters. The first node that is inspected by the algorithm is, evidently, the root of the parallel R*-tree. Note that at this stage (and until the first k objects are visited) there is no available information concerning the upper bound for the distance to the k-th nearest neighbor. Let in the current node N reside m MBRs, pointing to m children nodes. The question is which of the m branches can be discarded (if any), and how can we obtain the needed information to perform the pruning. In order to proceed, we need to calculate a threshold distance. The following lemma explains:

Lemma 7.1
Assume we have m MBRs $R_1, ..., R_m$ where MBR R_j contains $O(R_j)$ objects. Given a query point P, the k nearest neighbors with respect to P are requested. Assume further that all m MBRs are sorted in increasing order with respect to the $MAXDIST$ distance from the query point P. Then, all k best answers are contained inside the circle (sphere, hyper-sphere) with center P and radius

$r = MAXDIST(P, R_x)$ where x is determined from the following inequality:

$$\sum_{j=1}^{x-1} O(R_j) \leq k \leq \sum_{j=1}^{x} O(R_j) \quad (7.1)$$

Proof (omitted) □

Using the above lemma we can always determine a threshold distance D_{th}. Having D_{th}, some of the m entries may be rejected immediately. An example is illustrated in Figure 7.2. The threshold distance in the example equals: $D_{th} = MAXDIST(P, R_1)$. It can be easily observed that MBR R_5 is rejected since the dotted circle is guaranteed to contain all the relevant answers, and R_5 does not intersect the circle. However, there are some MBRs like R_2, R_3 and R_4, which are intersected by the circle. Therefore, the set of candidate MBRs is composed of R_1, R_2, R_3 and R_4. The problem arising is which of these candidates will be searched in the next step and which will be saved for future reference.

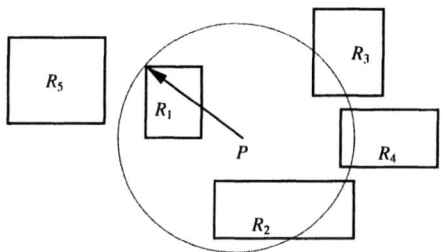

Figure 7.2. Illustration of pruning and candidate selection.

Assume in general that m_1 out of m entries have been pruned (like R_5 in the example). Now, we have $m_2 = m - m_1$ entries that need further inspection. The most straightforward approach is to assume that all these m_2 entries will eventually contribute to the final answer and therefore have to be searched. This technique is the main idea of the **Full Parallel Similarity Search** algorithm (**FPSS**), which is very optimistic with respect to the usefulness of a node.

2.3 Candidate Reduction Similarity Search

Instead, we propose to apply a heuristic here to (possibly) reduce the number of candidate MBRs. When observing Figure 7.2, it seems that MBR R_2 has better chances to contain relevant objects than MBRs R_3 and R_4. Therefore, candidates R_3 and R_4 are saved for future reference, whereas R_1 and R_2 will be searched. The criterion for candidate reduction has as follows:

Candidate Reduction Criterion
Given a query point P, a threshold distance D_{th} and a set of MBRs $\mathcal{R} = \{R_1, ..., R_m\}$ then for an MBR R_x:

(i) if $D_{th} < MINDIST(P, R_x)$, then R_x is rejected.

(ii) if $D_{th} \geq MINMAXDIST(P, R_x)$, then R_x is set active.

(iii) if $D_{th} \geq MINDIST(P, R_x)$ and $D_{th} < MINMAXDIST(P, R_x)$, then R_x is saved for possible future reference. □

The activation list contains the addresses to all nodes that are going to be requested from the disks in the current step. Each entry contains a pointer to its son. This means that we can fetch the nodes pointed by R_1 and R_2 from the disk array (if these nodes reside on different disks this can be done in parallel). Notice that up to now, no real object has been visited. As soon as the first k objects are retrieved, we have a more precise knowledge regarding the distance D_k from the query point P to its k-th nearest neighbor. Every time the distance D_k is updated due to access of data objects, the structure maintaining the remaining candidate MBRs is searched and new MBRs become active. The algorithm that is obtained from the application of the heuristic is called **C**andidate **R**eduction **S**imilarity **S**earch (**CRSS**).

Evidently, for the **CRSS** method to work, some auxiliary data structures need to be maintained. Based on the previous discussion we can identify three auxiliary structures:

- a structure to maintain the pointers to the nodes that are going to be fetched in the next step (activation structure),

- a structure to hold the newly fetched nodes to process them further (fetch structure), and

- a structure to store the candidate MBRs that have neither been searched nor have they been rejected yet (candidate structure).

The structures for (i) and (ii) can be simple arrays or linked lists and no special treatment is required. As soon as the currently relevant pointers (node addresses) have been collected in the activation structure, requests are sent to the corresponding disks to access the required nodes. When the disks have processed the requests, the nodes are collected in the fetch structure where further processing (pruning, candidate reduction, etc.) can be performed. The auxiliary structure to store the candidate MBRs must however be a stack, with its entries organized in a convenient way that helps processing. The cooperation of all three structures is explained in the following illustrative example.

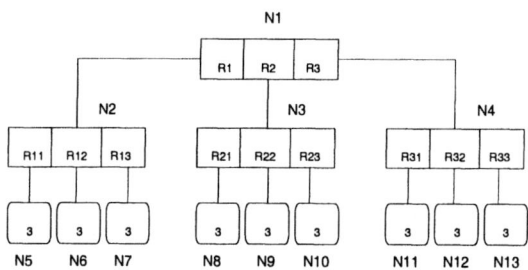

Figure 7.3. Example of an R*-tree with 13 nodes and 3 entries per node.

Example

An R*-tree is illustrated in Figure 7.3, where all tree nodes are assumed to hold three occupied entries. Nodes are numbered from N_1 to N_{13}. Let us trace the execution **CRSS** algorithm for a simple query requiring the $k = 4$ nearest neighbors of a query point.

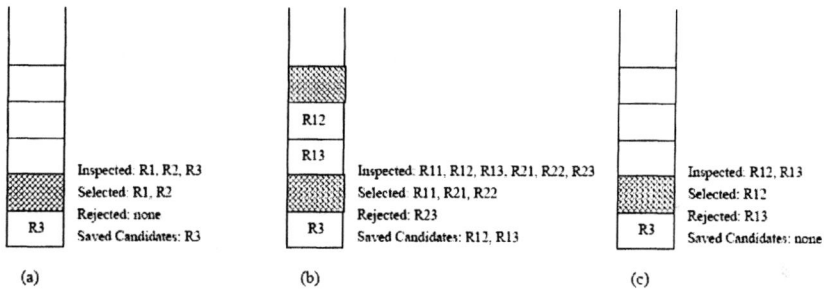

Figure 7.4. Illustration of the first three stages of the **CRSS** algorithm. Different candidate runs are separated by guards, indicated by shaded boxes.

The algorithm begins with the root (node $N1$) where the MBRs R_1, R_2 and R_3 reside. Assume that R_1 and R_2 qualify for immediate activation (according to the candidate reduction criterion), whereas R_3 is considered as a possible candidate MBR. No MBR is being rejected here. The pointers to the nodes N_2 and N_3 are maintained in the activation structure and MBR R_3 is pushed into the candidate stack. Note that the candidates are pushed in decreasing order with respect to the $MINDIST$ from the query point. After the stack is updated, we are ready to fetch nodes N_2 and N_3 from the disks. Assume that these two nodes reside in different disks and therefore the requests can be serviced in parallel. The situation is depicted in Figure 7.4(a).

In the next step, entries R_{11} through R_{23} are inspected. Assume that we have concluded that entry R_{23} is rejected, R_{11}, R_{21} and R_{22} will be activated, and finally R_{12} and R_{13} will be saved in the stack. The situation is illustrated in Figure 7.4(b).

The following stage involves the access of the data nodes N_5, N_8 and N_9. This is the first time during the execution of the algorithm that real data objects contribute to the formulation of the upper bound to the k-th best distance (where $k=4$). Therefore, the best 4 out of 9 objects, contained in the 3 data pages, are selected and the distance D_{th} is updated accordingly. Now we pop from the stack the first candidate run that is composed of the MBRs R_{12} and R_{13}. After comparing $MINDIST(P, R_{12})$ and $MINDIST(P, R_{13})$ with D_{th}, we conclude that R_{12} is intersected by the query sphere, whereas R_{13} can be safely rejected. The current situation is depicted in Figure 7.4(c).

In the next step, node N_6 is accessed, the distance D_{th} is updated and the next candidate run is popped from the stack. This run contains only R_3. Comparing $MINDIST(P, R_3)$ with D_{th}, we find that there is no intersection with the query sphere and therefore R_3 is rejected from further consideration. Now the algorithm has been terminated, the best k matches have been determined and $D_{th}=D_k$. □

Let us explain the use of the stack, and why is the appropriate structure in our case. As we descent the tree from root to leaves, the granularity of MBRs increases, since the empty space is reduced. Therefore, the information obtained from the MBRs near the leaf level is more precise than the information obtained from MBRs near the root. It is not wise to start the inspection of a new branch in a higher R*-tree level, if there are still candidate branches to be inspected in a lower level. The structure that captures this concept is the stack. Therefore, using a stack, candidate MBRs that belong to a high level are pushed in the stack before candidates of a lower level. Moreover, organizing the candidates in the stack by means of candidate runs, helps in pruning. The candidates in each run are sorted in increasing order with respect to the $MINDIST$ distance from the query point. When a candidate run is inspected and a candidate is found that does not intersect any more the query sphere, we know that all the remaining candidates in the current run should be rejected from further consideration. A guard entry is used to separate two different candidate runs. This technique saves computational power during candidate elimination and leads to faster processing.

In Figure 7.5 the **CRSS** algorithm is sketched. There are four basic operating modes that the algorithm can be at some given time:

- The algorithm operates in **ADAPTIVE** mode from the time the root is examined until the leaf level is reached for the first time. During this period, the upper bound of the threshold distance D_{th} is adapted when passing from one tree level to the next one. When the algorithm leaves this mode, it never goes into it again during the remaining part of the execution.

Multidisk Query Processing

```
                    Algorithm CRSS
Input:  P /* query point */
        k /* number of nearest neighbors */
        T /* a parallel R*-tree */
Output: k nearest neighbors of P
Init:   D_th = Inf, mode=ADAPTIVE,
        AL=EMPTY, CS=EMPTY, FL=EMPTY

1. Read Root(T) and place MBRs in FL;
2. If (leaf-level reached) set mode=UPDATE;
3. Process(FL);
4. if (mode is not TERMINATE)
   {
     Access nodes that have been recorded
     in AL structure;
     GOTO 2;
   }
   else STOP;

/*
Routine to obtain the next candidate run from the
Candidate Stack (CS)
*/
Get_Candidate_Run (CS)
{
  if (no candidate run exists)
  {
    set mode=TERMINATE;
    return;
  }
  else
  {
    pop next candidate run from CS;       ⎤
    eliminate non-relevant MBRs;          ⎬ B
    place relevant MBRs into AL;          ⎦
    set mode=NORMAL;
    return;
  }
}

/*
Routine to process a number of newly fetched
MBRs. After returning the addresses of the needed
nodes reside in the AL structure. */
Process (FL)
{
  if (mode is ADAPTIVE)
  {
    find new value for D_th;              ⎤
    formulate new canidate run;           ⎬ A
    push run into CS;                     ⎦
  }
  else
  if (mode is NORMAL)
  {
    eliminate non-relevant MBRs;
    if (FL is EMPTY)
    {
      Get_Candidate_Run (CS);
      Place elevant MBRs into AL;
    }
  }
  else
  if (mode is UPDATE)
  {
    calculate new set of nearest-neighbors;
    Get_Candidate_Run (CS);
  }
}
```

Figure 7.5. The most important code fragments of the **CRSS** algorithm.

- Every time the leaf level is reached, the algorithm goes into **UPDATE** mode. This means that the array holding the current best k distances is (possibly) updated, since more data objects have been accessed.

- In any other case, the algorithm operates in **NORMAL** mode. This mode includes the cases where the algorithm operates in an intermediate tree level but after the first time the leaf level is reached.

- Finally, the **TERMINATE** mode signals that there are no more candidate nodes to be searched, and therefore the k best distances have been determined.

It is observed that **FPSS** and **BBSS** are special cases of the **CRSS** algorithm. **FPSS** does not use a candidate stack and activates all MBRs that intersect the current query sphere, maximizing intraquery parallelism, whereas **BBSS** activates the MBRs one at a time, limiting the degree of intraquery parallelism. Let us elaborate more in code fragments **A** and **B** shown in Figure 7.5. In **A**, the candidate reduction criterion is applied. Among the fetched MBRs, some of them are discarded immediately, and some will be saved in the candidate stack for future reference. The restriction applied here is that the number of activated MBRs should be $\geq l$ and $\leq u$, where l is the number of MBRs which guarantee the containment of at least k points in the activated MBRs, and u equals the number of disks in the system ($NumOfDisks$). This restriction is used to bound the number of fetched nodes in the next step. A similar policy is used in the **B** code fragment. Here, the candidate reduction criterion is again applied. When there is a need to pop the next candidate run from the stack, we never allow the activation of more than $u=NumOfDisks$ elements. Using this technique, there is a balance between parallelism exploitation and similarity search refinement. Keep in mind however, that this technique needs a good declustering scheme. In order for the u MBRs to reside in different disks, the declustering scheme must be as close to optimal as possible.

We close this subsection by providing a theorem which shows that the **CRSS** algorithm is correct:

Theorem 7.1
Given a query point P and a number k, algorithm **CRSS** reports the best k nearest neighbors of P.

Proof
Basically, the algorithm can be considered as a repetition of three steps: (i) candidate elimination, (ii) generation of new candidates and (iii) retrieval of new data. Since the threshold distance D_{th} guarantees the inclusion of the best answers (Lemma 7.1) and only irrelevant MBRs are eliminated (according to the candidate reduction criterion), it is impossible that a best match will be missed. Moreover, the algorithm reports exactly k answers, unless the total number of objects in the database is less than k, in which case reports all the objects. □

2.4 Optimal Similarity Search

Designing an algorithm for similarity search we need a criterion to characterize the algorithm as efficient or inefficient. The ideal would be to design an optimal algorithm, guaranteeing the best possible performance. In the context of similarity search, two levels of optimality are identified: **weak** and **strict** which are defined as follows.

Definition 7.2
A similarity search algorithm is called **weak-optimal**, if for every k-NN query the only nodes that are accessed are those that are intersected by the sphere having center the query point and radius the distance to the k-th nearest neighbor. □

Definition 7.3
A similarity search algorithm is called **strict-optimal**, if it is weak-optimal, and in addition for every k-NN query the only objects that are inspected lie in the sphere with center the query point and radius the distance to the k-th nearest neighbor. □

It is evident that for an algorithm to be either weak-optimal or strict-optimal, the distance from the query point to the k-th nearest neighbor must be known in advance. Moreover, in strict optimality the algorithm must also process only the objects that are enclosed by the sphere with center P and radius D_k. This implies a special organization of the data objects and it is rather impossible to achieve strict optimality in similarity search. Also, although weak optimality still imposes a strong assumption, we assume the existence of a hypothetical algorithm Weak OPTimal Similarity Search (**WOPTSS**), and we include it in our experimental evaluation. The performance of **WOPTSS** method serves as a lower bound for the performance of any similarity search algorithm. The following theorem illustrates that the algorithms presented previously are not optimal:

Theorem 7.2
The similarity search algorithms **BBSS**, **FPSS** and **CRSS** operating over an R*-tree, are neither strict-optimal nor weak-optimal.

Proof (sketch)
We can find a counterexample for all algorithms with respect to certain query points and R*-tree layouts, showing that neither the minimum number of nodes are visited, nor the minimum number of objects are inspected. □

The number of accessed nodes is a good metric for the performance of a similarity search algorithm in the sequential case. However, in the parallel case the situation is more complicated. When processing similarity queries on a disk array, one wants high parallelism exploitation in addition to small number of accesses. A more concrete measure of efficiency in this case is the response time of a similarity query in a multiuser environment. Evidently, one can use the response time of a single query but this does not reflect reality. To see why, assume that an algorithm A accesses half of the pages with respect to algorithm B. On a disk array, the I/O subsystem is capable of servicing several requests in parallel. Therefore, we may notice no difference in the response time of a single query for both algorithms, whereas in a multiuser environment the performance of algorithm B is more likely to degrade rapidly in comparison to the performance of A, due to heavy workloads. The question we are going to answer in the subsequent section is the following: *Which of the three proposed algorithms performs the best in a multiuser environment, and how fast this algorithm processes similarity queries in comparison to the* **WOPTSS** *method?*

3. Performance Evaluation

3.1 Preliminaries

The algorithms **BBSS**, **FPSS**, **CRSS** and **WOPTSS** are implemented on top of a parallel R*-tree structure which is distributed among the components of a disk array. The behavior of the system is studied using event-driven simulation. The algorithms and the simulator have been coded in C/C++ under UNIX, and the experiments have been performed on a SUN Sparcstation4 running Solaris 2.4.

The data sets that are used to perform the performance comparison of the algorithms include real-life as well as synthetic ones. Obviously, many different data sets could be included in our study. Among the data sets we have used for the experiments, the most representative ones are illustrated in the following figures.

The upper part of Figure 7.6 presents the real-life data sets that are selected from the Sequoia 2000 (California places - CP) [128] and the TIGER project (Long Beach –LB) [138]. The CP data set is composed of 62,173 2-d points representing locations of various California places. The LB data set consists of 53,145 2-d points representing road segment intersections in Long Beach county. The lower part of Figure 7.6 presents two of the synthetic data sets that have been used. The SG set is composed of a number of points distributed with respect to the Gaussian (normal) distribution. The SU set consists of a number of points obeying the uniform distribution. The population and the dimensionality of the synthetic data sets were varying during the experiments. In the figure, their 2-d counterparts are illustrated, containing 10,000 points each. However, values up to 300,000 points have been used in the experimentation.

Multidisk Query Processing

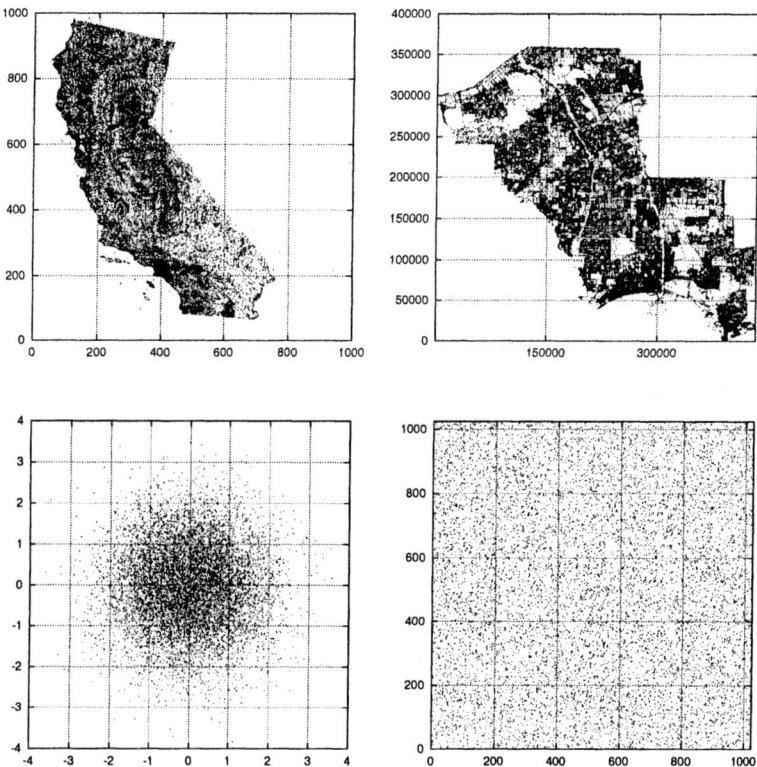

Figure 7.6. Datasets used in performance evaluation.

An R*-tree for a particular data set is constructed incrementally (i.e. by inserting the objects one-by-one). The disks are assumed to communicate with the processor by means of a common I/O bus. The network queue model of the system that is used for the simulation is presented in Figure 7.7. Each disk has its own queue where pending requests are appended. The service policy for each queue in the system is FCFS (First-Come First-Served). The bus is also modeled as a queue, with constant service time (the time it takes to transmit a page from the disk controller through the I/O bus). Queues are also present in the processor to handle pending requests. However, we assume that when a new query request arrives, it enters the system immediately without waiting.

It is evident that in a common bus, only one transmission at a time can take place. Therefore, if two disk controllers demand access to the I/O bus simultaneously, only one can do so. If other devices are attached on the same

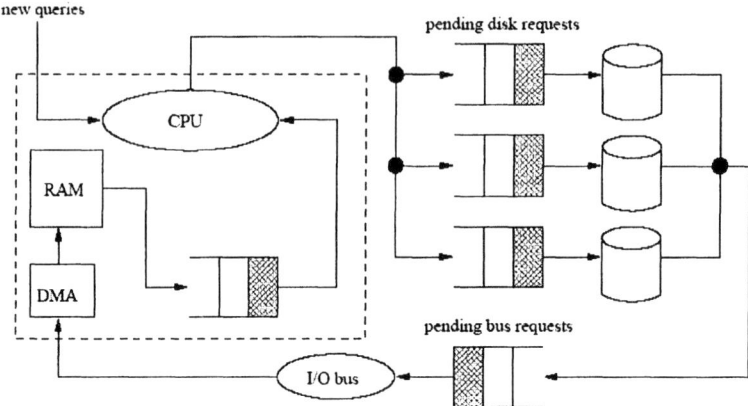

Figure 7.7. The simulation model for the system under consideration.

I/O bus, then we may have other (interdevice) conflicts as well. However, in our study we take into consideration only the conflicts due to the disk array components ignoring interdevice conflicts, anticipating that the impact of the latter on the performance comparison is more or less the same for all studied algorithms.

Query arrivals follow a Poisson distribution with mean λ arrivals per second. Therefore, the query interarrival time interval is a random variable following an exponential distribution. The service time for the bus is constant, whereas the service time of a disk access is calculated taking into consideration the most important disk characteristics (seek time, rotational latency, transfer time and controller overhead). Moreover, we do not assume that the disks are synchronized, and therefore each disk can move its heads independently from the others. The parameter values that are used in the experimental evaluation are presented in Table 7.1.

In order to model each disk device, the two-phase non-linear model is used which is described in detail in [71, 108]. If d_{seek} denotes the seek distance that the head needs to travel, the seek time T_{seek} as a function of d_{seek} is expressed by the following equation:

$$T_{seek} = \begin{cases} 0, & d_{seek} = 0 \quad \text{(no seek)} \\ c_1 + c_2 \cdot \sqrt{d_{seek}}, & 0 < d_{seek} \leq cutoff \quad \text{(short seek)} \\ c_3 + c_4 \cdot d_{seek}, & d_{seek} > cutoff \quad \text{(long seek)} \end{cases}$$

where c_1, c_2, c_3 and c_4 are constants (in msecs) specific to the disk drive used and $cutoff$ is a seek distance value, which differentiates the acceleration phase and

Parameter	Description	Assigned Value
S_{node}	Node capacity	4 KB
n	Space dimensionality	2 to 30
N	Number of objects	>10,000
k	Number of nearest neighbors	1 to 700
d	Number of disks	1 to 40
λ	Query arrivals per second	≤ 30
B	I/O bus bandwidth	20 MB/sec
CPU_{speed}	CPU execution speed	100 MIPS
$Q_{startup}$	Query startup time	0.001 sec

Table 7.1. Description of query processing parameters.

the steady-speed phase of the disk arm movement. The disk drive characteristics that is used in the conducted simulation experiments are illustrated in Table 7.2.

Parameter	Description	Assigned Value
Cyl	number of cylinders	1449
T_{rev}	disk revolution time	0.0149 sec
R_{trans}	disk transfer rate	5 MB/sec
T_{seek}	disk seek time	variable
O_{ctrl}	disk controller overhead	0.0011 sec
c_1	short-seek constant 1	3.45 msec
c_2	short-seek constant 2	0.597 msec
c_3	long-seek constant 1	10.8 msec
c_4	long-seek constant 2	0.012 msec
$cutoff$	threshold seek distance	616

Table 7.2. Description of disk characteristics (model HP-C220A) [108].

During R*-tree creation, each newly generated node (after a split operation) is assigned a cylinder value with respect to the uniform distribution. Evidently this is not the best possible allocation strategy, since it does not respect locality. Placing pages that are referenced together on the same cylinder reduces the disk service times and this effect is orthogonal with respect to the similarity search algorithms, with the difference that response times are reduced. Initially, all disk arms are positioned in cylinder zero. The simulator executes 100 queries in total, and the response time per query is obtained by calculating the average.

With respect to CPU execution costs, it is assumed that computation time is dominated by the scanning and sorting of each requested set of MBRs. Assume that N MBRs have been fetched from the disks. The scanning of these MBRs costs $O(N)$ time. After scanning, some of them are rejected so that M MBRs remain in the sequel. In order to sort M elements, the computational effort is $O(M \cdot logM)$ comparisons (assuming heapsort or mergesort). Each main memory word has four bytes and also each number is modeled as four bytes of main memory. Fetching a number from main memory requires one CPU instruction. Therefore, to compare two numbers, three CPU instructions are required (two for fetching the operands and one for the comparison). Thus, the computation cost for scanning equals $2 \cdot N$ CPU instructions and the computation time for sorting is equivalent to executing $3 \cdot M \cdot logM$ CPU instructions, resulting in a total of $2 \cdot N + 3 \cdot M \cdot logM$ CPU instructions. Since the MIPS rate for the CPU is a known parameter, the computation time is easily calculated. Although this cost model is simple, it reflects the CPU overhead to a sufficient degree. Considering more complex computation models leads to more accurate simulation results, but the impact on the comparison of similarity search algorithms is negligible. Having described the cost model for all the fundamental simulator components, we continue with the illustration of some representative performance results.

3.2 Experimental Results

Evidently, it is very difficult to provide experimental results by modifying all parameter values. Therefore, we choose to illustrate representative results that shed light in the following interesting issues:

- Effectiveness: how many nodes an algorithm visits to produce the final answer in comparison to the **WOPTSS** method,

- Speed-up: how the performance of the methods is affected by increasing the number of disk array units,

- The impact of query size and dimensionality: how the algorithms perform with increasing query size and/or space dimensionality,

Multidisk Query Processing

- The impact of workload: what is the behavior of the methods when concurrent queries are serviced by the system.

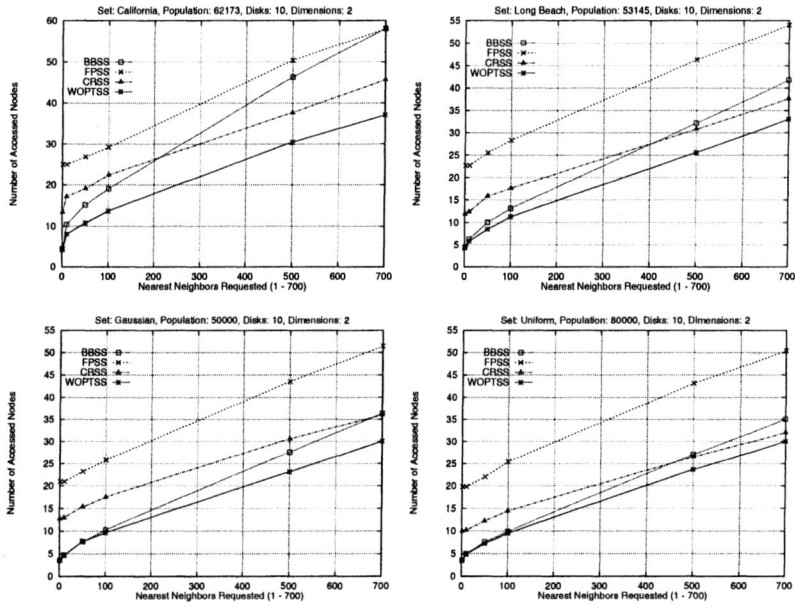

Figure 7.8. Number of visited nodes vs. query size for 2-d data sets.

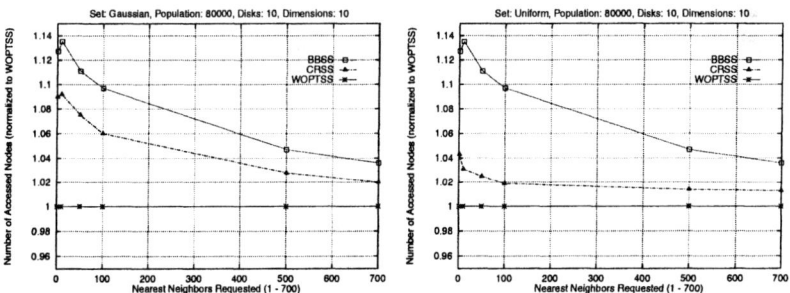

Figure 7.9. Number of visited nodes (normalized to **WOPTSS**) vs. query size for synthetic data in 10-d space.

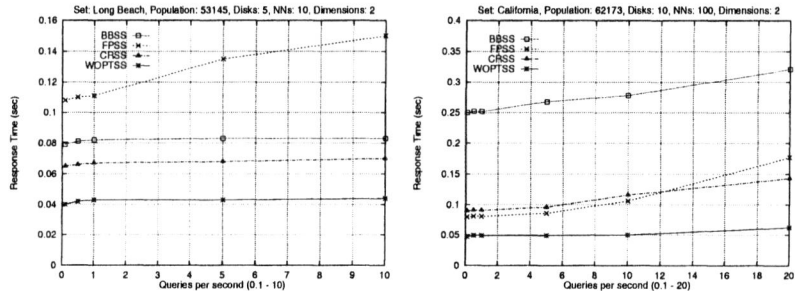

Figure 7.10. Response time (secs) vs. query arrival rate (λ).

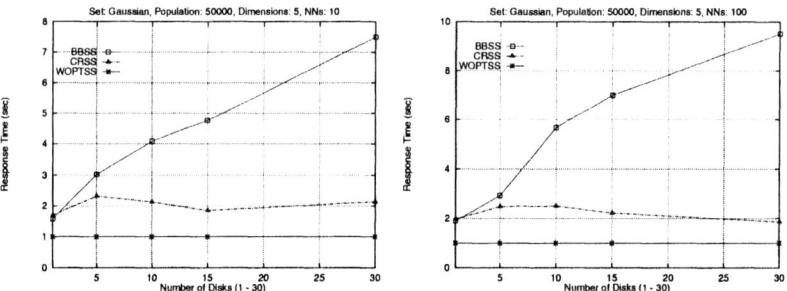

Figure 7.11. Response time (normalized to WOPTSS) vs. number of disks (λ=5 queries/sec, dimensions=5).

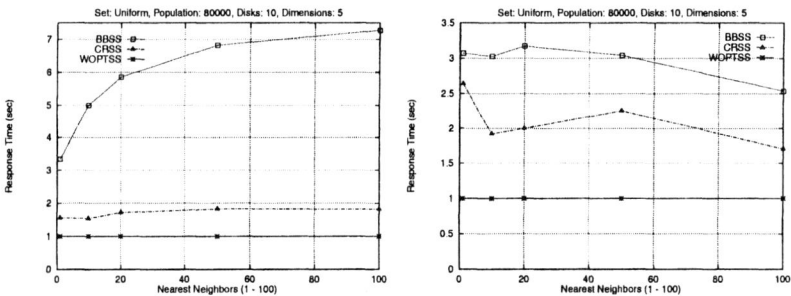

Figure 7.12. Response time (normalized to **WOPTSS**) vs. number of nearest neighbors (Left: λ=1 queries/sec, Right: λ=20 queries/sec).

Multidisk Query Processing 105

Population	Disks	BBSS	CRSS	WOPTSS
10,000	5	0.76	0.47	0.23
20,000	10	0.74	0.28	0.15
40,000	20	1.07	0.29	0.15
80,000	40	1.59	0.33	0.16

Table 7.3. Scalability with respect to population growth: Response time (secs) vs. population and number of disks. (set: gaussian, dimensions: 5, NNs: 20, λ=5 queries/sec).

k	Disks	BBSS	CRSS	WOPTSS
10	5	2.48	1.30	0.48
20	10	2.14	0.32	0.19
40	20	2.37	0.55	0.28
80	40	2.95	0.40	0.21

Table 7.4. Scalability with respect to query size growth: Response time (secs) vs. number of nearest neighbors and number of disks. (set: gaussian, dimensions: 5, population: 80,000, λ=5 queries/sec).

3.3 Interpretation of Results

By inspecting Figures 7.8 - 7.12 and Tables 7.3 - 7.4 some very interesting observations can be stated. As expected, **WOPTSS** shows the best performance in all experiments contacted. With respect to effectiveness (see Figure 7.8 - 7.9), **BBSS** fetches the smaller number of nodes up to a point. After this point, **CRSS** is more effective, and the performance of **BBSS** deteriorates by increasing the number of nearest neighbors. In order to explain this behavior of **BBSS** a small example is given in Figure 7.13, assuming that $k = 12$. Since the algorithm chooses to visit the MBR with the smallest $MINDIST$ distance, MBR R_1 will be visited first. If 12 data objects lie in the subtree of R_1, all of them will be visited, despite the fact that some of them will not contribute to the final answer. Evidently, in the branch of R_2 lie some objects that are closer to the query point. Therefore, if R_1 and R_2 were visited in a BFS (Breadth First Search) manner, the total number of disk accesses could have been reduced

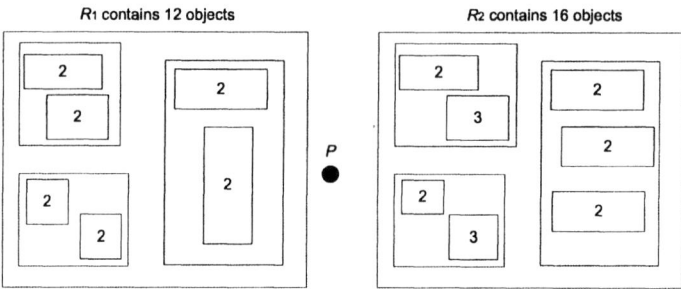

Figure 7.13. **BBSS** will visit all nodes associated with the branch of R_1, leading to unnecessary accesses.

considerably. The drawback of **BBSS** affects its performance even more, by increasing the number of dimensions, as shown in Figure 7.9. By increasing the space dimensionality, the overlap of the MBRs increases also, and therefore the pruning of branches becomes a difficult task. Moreover, several MBRs may have zero value for the $MINDIST$ distance, resulting in a difficulty to select the appropriate next branch to follow. The superiority of **CRSS** lies in the fact that it uses a successful combination of BFS and DFS (Depth First Search) of the parallel R*-tree. On the other hand, **BBSS** is DFS-based, whereas **FPSS** is BFS-based. Algorithm **FPSS** fails to control the number of fetched nodes and this results in a large number of disk accesses. The good performance of **CRSS** is retained in all data sets used and all examined dimensionalities.

In Figure 7.10, we illustrate the response time per query versus the query arrival rate. **FPSS** is very sensitive in workload increase, since there is no control on the number of fetched nodes. Its performance is the worst in comparison to the other methods. However, for small workloads and large number of disks **FPSS** is marginally better than **CRSS**. This is illustrated in Figure 7.10 (right graph). This happens because the large number of disks compensates the increased demand for disk accesses.

Figure 7.11 demonstrates response time versus number of disks. It is evident that the speed-up of **CRSS** is better than that of **BBSS**. In fact **CRSS** is between 2 to 4 times faster than **BBSS**. Algorithm **FPSS** is not considered any more, since its performance is very sensitive on the workload and the number of disks in the system.

The performance of the methods with respect to the number of nearest neighbors is illustrated in Figure 7.12. Again, it is observed that **CRSS** shows the best performance, outperforming **BBSS** by factors (3 to 4 times faster). Finally, Tables 7.3 and 7.4 present the scalability of the algorithms with respect to population growth and query size growth. **CRSS** is more stable than **BBSS** and on average is 4 times faster.

The general conclusion derived is that **CRSS** is on average 2 times slower than **WOPTSS** and outperforms by factors both **BBSS** and **FPSS**. Thus, **CRSS** succeeds in:

- fetching a small number of nodes, and
- exploiting parallelism to a sufficient degree.

For these reasons, the use of **CRSS** is recommended as a fast and simple similarity search algorithm in a system based on disk arrays. Table 7.5 contains a qualitative comparison of the studied algorithms, summarizing the performance evaluation results.

	BBSS	FPSS	CRSS	WOPTSS
disk accesses	√		√	√
throughput			√	√
response time			√	√
speed-up		√	√	√
scalability			√	√
intraquery I/O parallelism		√	√	√
interquery I/O parallelism	√	limited	√	√

Table 7.5. Qualitative comparison of all algorithms (a √ means good performance).

4. Summary

The problem of exploiting I/O parallelism in database systems is a major research direction. In this chapter, we investigated similarity search techniques for disk arrays. The fundamental properties that such an algorithm should preserve are: parallelism must be exploited as much as possible, the total resource consumption should be minimized, the response time of user queries should be reduced as much as possible and throughput must be maximized.

Three possible similarity search techniques are presented and studied in detail with respect to the above issues. Moreover, an optimal approach (**WOPTSS**) is defined, which assumes that the distance D_k from the query point to the k-th nearest neighbor is known in advance, and therefore only the relevant nodes are inspected. Unfortunately, this algorithm is hypothetical, since the distance D_k is generally not known. However, useful lower bounds are derived by studying the behavior of the optimal method. All methods are studied under extensive experimentation through simulation. The simulation process takes into consideration the disk model, the conflicts on the I/O bus, and CPU time. A number of different datasets are used with various populations, distributions and dimensionalities. Among the studied algorithms, the proposed one (**CRSS**) which is based on a careful inspection of the R*-tree nodes, and leads to an effective candidate reduction, shows the best performance. However, the performance difference between **CRSS** and **WOPTSS** suggests that further research is required to reach the lower bound as much as possible.

5. Further Reading

The exploitation of multiple disk units for efficient query processing has been studied in [113] in the case of B-trees. In [141] the authors study optimal methods for data declustering, by using a closed-form formula to estimate the performance of the methods. In [11] the authors propose an efficient technique for parallel query processing in high-dimensional spaces. Efficient methods for parallel query processing using M-trees have been proposed in [147].

Chapter 8

MULTIPROCESSOR QUERY PROCESSING

1. Introduction

In Chapter 6 we discussed some important issues regarding the exploitation of multiple processors towards increased query processing efficiency. In this chapter we continue with a performance evaluation of parallel NN algorithms in a parallel database system, which is supported by a set of interconnected computer systems (network of workstations). The challenge in this case is to partition the data among the several processors to achieve good performance during query processing. In addition, the query processor must be carefully designed, taking into consideration that processor communication is performed by message passing, and therefore data transfer costs are not negligible.

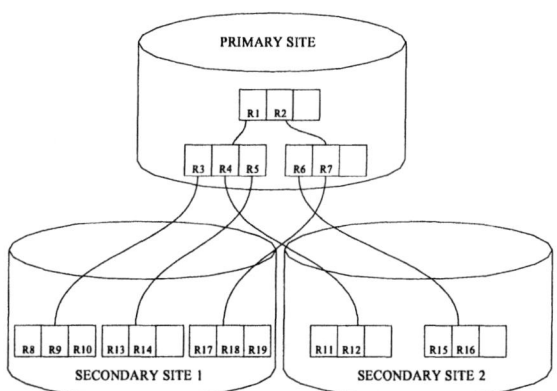

Figure 8.1. Declustering an R-tree over three sites.

Given that the dataset is known in advance, Koudas et. al. suggest sorting the data with respect to the Hilbert values of the MBR centroids [58]. Then, the tree leaf level is formed and the assignment of leaves to sites is performed in a round-robin manner. This method guarantees that leaves that contain objects close in the address space will be assigned to different sites, thus increasing the parallelism during range query processing. In Figure 8.1 we present a way to decluster an R-tree in three sites, one primary and two secondary.

Recall that although in this study we assume that the processors reside in different computer systems, the methodology can be applied to more tightly-coupled architectures as well, where processors reside in the same machine.

The material of this chapter is based on [92, 94] and is organized as follows. In the next section we present some performance estimation issues which are used throughout the chapter to predict the number of disk accesses for a k-NN query. Section 3 studies NN query processing algorithms, whereas Section 4 contains the performance evaluation results of the study.

2. Performance Estimation

In this section we show how we can estimate the number of leaf accesses involved due to the processing of a k-NN query. In Chapter 4 we gave average upper and lower bounds with respect to the number of leaf accesses for $k=1$ NN queries only, assuming that the query points are allowed to "land" on actual data points only. In this chapter, we are based on a different query model, which assumes a uniform distribution of the query points over the whole address space. The latter model, even if it does not reflect reality always, it has been used by many researchers working in the access methods area [87]. Here we try to estimate this number as precisely as possible, using statistical information that we assume are available. The estimation of the number of leaf accesses is based on the following basic observation to which we have concluded after conducting a series of experiments. The analytical derivation of a closed formed formula to verify the validity of this observation is an issue for further research.

Basic Observation

If the query points follow a uniform distribution over the 2-d data space, then the average number of R-tree leaf accesses involved when we process a k-NN query, using the branch-and-bound algorithm, grows almost linearly with respect to k. □

This linearity property allow us to approximate the expected number of leaf accesses using a linear equation of the form:

$$F(k) = a * k + b \qquad (8.1)$$

where k is the number of nearest neighbors, $F(k)$ the expected number of leaf accesses, a the curve slope and b a real positive constant. The main problem is to calculate a and b. We can base the calculation on available statistical information. Let us assume that we have the expected number of leaf accesses $F(k_1)$ and $F(k_2)$ for k_1 and k_2 nearest neighbors, respectively, where $k_1 \neq k_2$. It is evident that:

$$a = \frac{F(k_2) - F(k_1)}{k_2 - k_1} \quad (8.2)$$

and

$$b = F(k_1) - a * k_1 \quad (8.3)$$

Using sample values for k_1 and k_2 we can measure the values $F(k_1)$ and $F(k_2)$. From Equations (8.2) and (8.3) we obtain the values for a and b respectively. Substituting in Equation (8.1) we have a formula to estimate the expected number of leaf accesses. The values k_1 and k_2 can be selected by the database administrator or can be adjusted by the statistical module. In our framework we used the values $k_1 = 10$ and $k_2 = 500$.

The graphs of Figure 8.2 show the measured and estimated number of leaf accesses versus the number k of nearest neighbors. The datasets used are described in a subsequent section. For each graph 100 NN queries were generated uniformly over the data space and the average number of leaf accesses was calculated. It is evident that the approximation is reasonably accurate (the maximum and mean errors are around 20% and 10% respectively) and therefore it can be used for estimation purposes. We also studied a regression based approximation using several sample values of k (k_1, k_2, ..., k_n). Although a more accurate estimation was obtained on average, the practical impact on the performance of the proposed algorithm was negligible.

3. Parallel Algorithms
3.1 Adapting BB-NNF in Declustered R-trees

In order to apply the **BB-NNF** method in a declustered R-tree, some modifications need to be considered. Recall that the data pages are searched one-by-one and consequently, each server is activated one-by-one. Because the determination of the best answers is performed through successive refinement, every time a new data page is searched, the current set of nearest neighbors is updated accordingly. This behavior results in two alternatives to process NN queries over a network.

BB-NNF-1

In this approach, when a new server is activated, the primary server sends the query point together with the currently best k distances. This way, the corresponding secondary server can determine the absolutely necessary

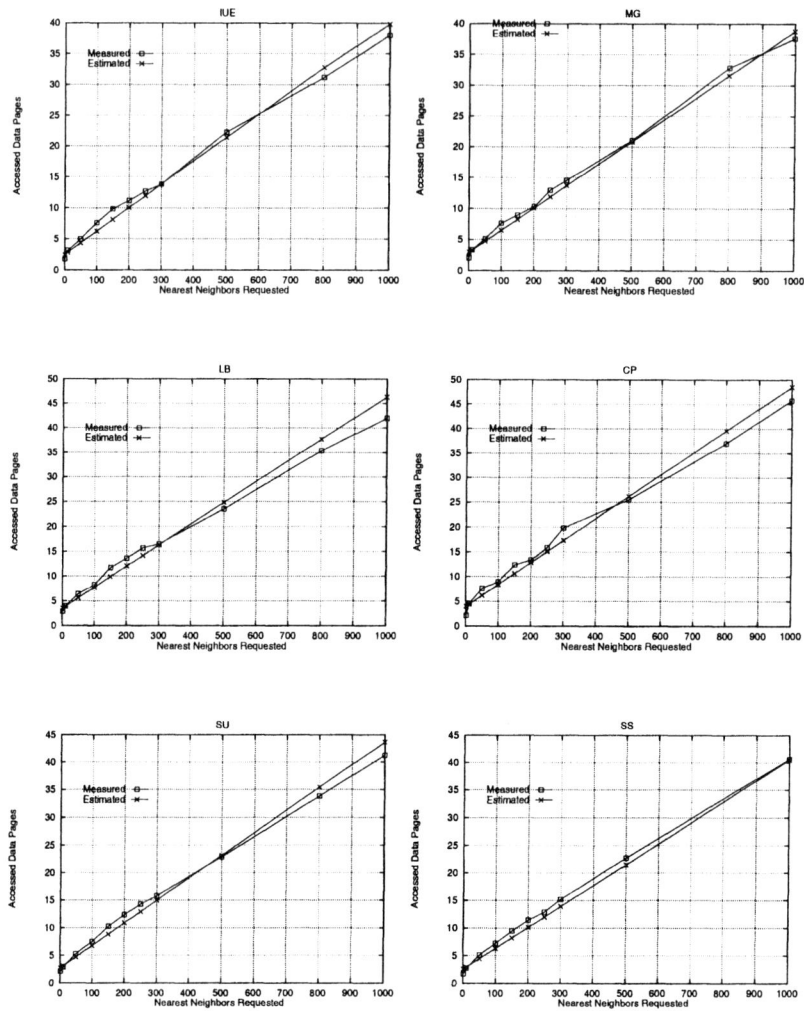

Figure 8.2. Measured and Estimated number of leaf accesses vs. the number k of nearest neighbors.

number of objects to transmit back. However, for large values of k, the network consumption can increase considerably and the benefits of this approach may be lost.

BB-NNF-2

In this approach, only the distance to the k-th currently best nearest neighbor of the query point is transmitted along with the query point itself. The advantage is that only few bytes are needed in order to activate a secondary site. On the other hand, the pruning that the activated secondary site can perform is limited, since the selection of the objects is performed with only one reference distance. Therefore, there is high probability that among the transmitted objects some of them are not necessary.

It is evident, that there is a trade off that need to be further investigated by means of experimental evaluation. In this respect, we consider both variants of **BB-NNF** for the comparison to be complete. The two approaches are based on the same concept but they differ in the implementation. In the sequel, when we mention **BB-NNF** we mean any of the two variants, if this does not pose confusion in readability.

3.2 The Parallel Nearest Neighbor Finding (P-NNF) Method

The main drawback of **BB-NNF** method is that due to its serial nature, query processing is not affected by the number of secondary sites available and therefore, no parallelism is exploited. Moreover, a particular site may be accessed several times, each time processing a different data page. Evidently, we would like to have more control on the processing strategy. Also, we would like to exploit parallelism as much as possible, thus speeding up processing. In this subsection we present and study the **P-NNF** method, suitable for answering NN queries in a declustered environment. In Figure 8.3, we illustrate the basic difference of the two methods.

In the top of the figure, we see how the **BB-NNF** method proceeds with the execution of a query. Each time a secondary server S_j is activated, the primary server must wait until the S_j transmits all the results. Then the primary server may proceed with the activation of another secondary server. All three phases, namely activation phase, local processing phase and result transmission phase, appear in a strict sequence and no parallel processing is achieved. On the other hand, as we present in the bottom of Figure 8.3, we would like to exploit parallelism during the local processing phase, reducing the query response time. Generally, each secondary server neither processes the same amount of data, nor transmits the same number of objects. The exact calculation of the response time and the cost model description is presented in Subsection 4.2.

In the sequel, we are using the distances $MINDIST$, $MINMAXDIST$ and $MAXDIST$ between a rectangle R and a point P, which have been defined in previous chapters. The distances are depicted in Figure 8.4. The main goal of the proposed method is to determine the secondary sites that are going to be activated simultaneously. The algorithm comprises of three different steps. First, we start at the primary site and we search the R-tree with respect to the $MINDIST$ measure from the query point, until the final internal tree level

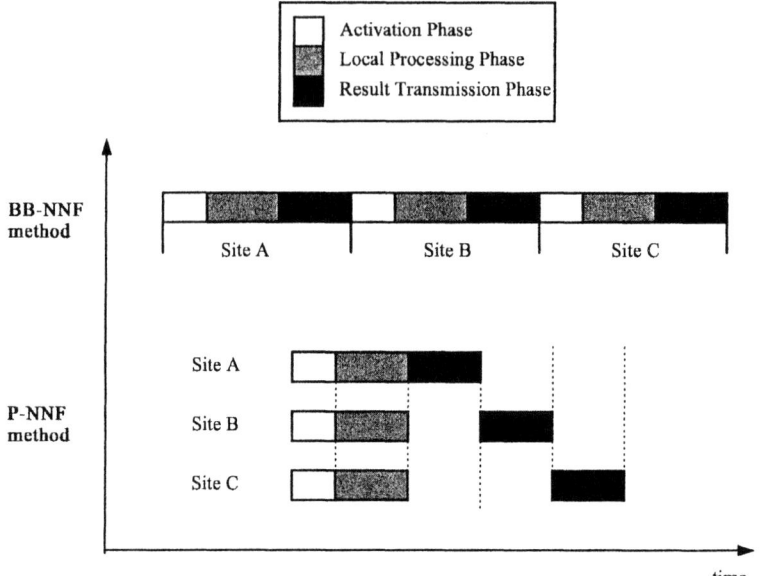

Figure 8.3. Basic difference between **BB-NNF** and **P-NNF** methods.

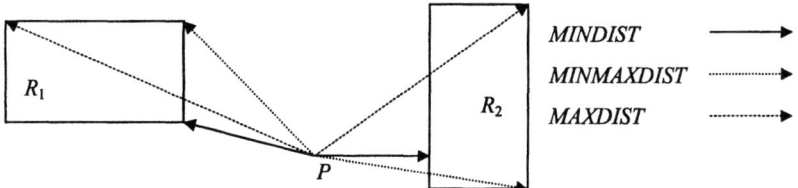

Figure 8.4. $MINDIST, MINMAXDIST$ and $MAXDIST$ between a point P and two rectangles R_1 and R_2.

(the "father" level of the data pages) is reached. In the second step, a radius D_r is determined which guarantees that all the qualifying objects (and other objects as well) are falling inside the circle with center the query point and radius D_r. Then, a range query is performed with respect to this circle and a set of data pages MBRs is gathered, by inspecting the MBRs of the last internal level. In the last step, the first $F(k)$ data pages (with respect to the $MINDIST$ metric) are visited and the relevant answers are collected. To guarantee the avoidance of dismissals, the remaining of the gathered MBRs must be checked for relevance. Bellow we describe each step of the algorithm in detail:

Algorithm P-NNF

Input: a query point P and the number k of nearest neighbors requested.

Output: a sorted sequence of distances $a_1, ..., a_k$ of the k nearest neighbors of P.

Step 1
Let the k nearest neighbors be requested with respect to a query point P. The R-tree is traversed top-down with respect to the $MINDIST$ metric. This means that, in each node we take the branch that corresponds to the MBR with the minimum $MINDIST$ with respect to the query point P. The traversal stops at the last R-tree internal level. Also, keep in mind that all upper levels are stored at the primary site, and all data pages are distributed in the available secondary sites. In this step no data pages are visited.

Step 2
Assume that the internal node I has been reached in **Step 1**. Let this node contain $e = O_{in}(I)$ entries, pointing to e data pages. We sort these pages in increasing order, with respect to the $MAXDIST$ metric and obtain the sorted sequence $B_1, ..., B_e$. Each data page B_j contains $O_{dp}(B_j)$ objects, where $1 \leq j \leq e$ and corresponds to a region $R(B_j)$ that encloses all the objects. Note that from node I at most $\sum_{j=1}^{e} O_{dp}(B_j)$ data objects can be accessed. Although we will generalize later, for the time being let $k \leq \sum_{j=1}^{e} O_{dp}(B_j)$. We determine the smallest positive integer c, where $1 \leq c \leq e$, such that the circle with center P and radius $D_r = MAXDIST(P, R(B_c))$ contains at least k objects. More formally:

$$\sum_{j=1}^{c} O_{db}(B_j) \geq k \geq \sum_{j=1}^{c-1} O_{db}(B_j)$$

A range query is performed in the R-tree, using the circle with center P and radius D_r and a set of data page MBRs is collected. Again, in this step, no data pages are accessed.

Step 3
Assume that M data page MBRs have been collected from the previous step. In general, this number is greater than the number of data pages we really need to obtain the answer. Here, we use the estimation for the expected number of leaf accesses illustrated in the previous subsection (see Equation (8.1)). Therefore, from the M MBRs we choose the first $m = F(k)$ with respect to the $MINDIST$ metric. The appropriate secondary sites are activated simultaneously, and the k most promising answers are collected.

If after the collection of the answers there are still MBRs, among the M, that may contain relevant objects, we must process them as well. Therefore, the $MINDIST$ of the remaining data page MBRs are compared with the k-th nearest neighbor of P. If for an MBR R the value of $MINDIST(P, R)$ is greater than the distance from P to its k-th nearest neighbor obtained so far, then R is rejected from consideration, since it is impossible to contain any of the nearest neighbors of P.

In Step 2 of the algorithm, we assumed that $k \leq \sum_{j=1}^{e} O_{dp}(B_j)$. In other words, from the first father node f_1 we visit, we can access at least k objects. However, it is possible that f_1 does not have enough occupied entries to cover k. The number of objects that are contained in each data page is recorded in the father node. Therefore, we know how many objects a data page contains, *before* visiting the page. The solution to this problem is very simple though. All we need is to visit another father f_2, with respect to the $MINDIST$ of the query point, such that the sum of the objects we can access from both f_1 and f_2, exceeds k. Evidently, this process can be continued with more father nodes, until the condition is satisfied.

3.3 When Statistics are not Available

In the previous subsections, we explained how the statistical information is exploited to process a NN query. However, statistics are not always available, and therefore there is a need to devise a modified **P-NNF** method to exploit parallelism, when statistics on the expected number of data page accesses are not available. The only difference of the new method (**P-NNF-2**) with **P-NNF** appears in **Step 3**. Recall that the number $F(k)$ (expected number of data page accesses) is used as an estimation for the relevant data pages, during searching for the k nearest neighbors of a query point P. However, in this case, the $F(k)$ value is not available, and some other starting point should be defined. Recall that, after the completion of **Step 2** of **P-NNF** algorithm, the M relevant MBRs of the data pages are sorted with respect to the $MINDIST$ distance from the query point. We determine an integer m_k such that:

$$\sum_{j=1}^{m_k} O_{dp}(B_j) \geq k \geq \sum_{j=1}^{m_k-1} O_{dp}(B_j)$$

In other words, we keep on investigating the sorted list, until the current sum of objects exceed the number k. Note that something similar has been performed in **Step 2** to determine the D_r distance. These first m_k data pages are guaranteed to contain at least k objects, but it is too optimistic to declare that all of the best objects will be among them. However, we hope that at least some of them will participate in the final answer, and that the rest will not be too far away from the query point, enabling effective pruning.

After the determination of m_k, the m_k data pages are accessed, and a sorted sequence $a_1, ..., a_k$ of the k best matches is formulated. Then, we check the $M - m_k$ remaining MBRs to determine if some of them need to be accessed. Therefore, all MBRs M_j where $MINDIST(P, M_j) \leq a_k$, should be further investigated. For this purpose, the primary site sends the sequence $a_1, ..., a_k$ to the relevant secondary sites, and collects the results. The primary server determines the best k objects, and formulates the final answer set of nearest neighbors.

3.4 Correctness of P-NNF Algorithms

One can observe that both **P-NNF** algorithms are correct. In other words, the methods determine a sorted list of object distances from the query point P, such that all k nearest neighbors of P are included. Let $a_1, ..., a_k$ be the sorted list of distance values. Without loss of generality, let $a_i \neq a_j$, where $1 \leq i, j \leq k$ and $i \neq j$. Assume that there is an object distance a_x that is not contained in the answer set, but for some j the following holds: $a_x < a_j$, where $1 \leq j \leq k$. This means that we have a false dismissal,, because an object that should be returned as one of the nearest neighbors, does not appear in the final answer. This can happen only due to one of the following reasons:

(i) The circular range query that is performed with respect to D_r distance does not cover all the best distances, or

(ii) A data page B_j is not visited, although $MINDIST(P, R(B_j)) \leq a'_k$, where a'_k is the currently best distance from P to its k-th nearest neighbor.

Case (i) is avoided, since D_r is selected in a way that encloses at least k objects. Case (ii) is avoided, since after the first formulation of the best distances $a'_1, ..., a'_k$, the remaining candidate data pages are checked with respect to the $MINDIST$ and a'_k. Therefore, any data page that may contain answers is accessed. Thus the following holds:

Proposition 8.1
Algorithms **P-NNF-1** and **P-NNF-2** are correct since they return at least k object distances $a_1, ..., a_k$ with respect to the query point P, and no distance smaller than a_k is left out. □

4. Performance Evaluation
4.1 Preliminaries

We implemented the Hilbert-packed R-tree, the branch-and-bound (**BB-NNF**) and the parallel nearest neighbor (**P-NNF**) algorithms in the C programming language under UNIX and simulate the parallel environment on a SUN

Sparcstation 4. The tree fanout is set to 50 and therefore, each node contains at most 50 entries.

The pure network speed, NS_{pure}, is set to 10Mbps. In order to investigate the behavior of the methods under different network loads, we make use of a variable $netload$ by which we divide the pure network speed and we get the effective network speed: $NS_{eff} = \frac{NS_{pure}}{netload}$. Due to the CSMA/CD protocol, many sites may try to transmit simultaneously, resulting in a collision. The net effect of the collisions is that there is a delay in transmitting a frame from a source to the destination. Therefore, the $netload$ variable reflects exactly this delay. We used the frame layout of the IEEE 802.3 CSMA/CD bus standard, which is illustrated in Figure 8.5. Both real-life and synthetic datasets have been used for the performance evaluation. The datasets are described in Table 8.1 and are shown graphically in Figure 8.6.

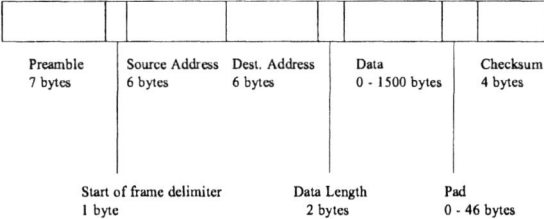

Figure 8.5. The IEEE 802.3 (CSMA/CD bus) frame layout.

Dataset	Population	Description
IUE	15,100	Star coordinates from International Ultraviolet Explorer (NASA)
MG	27,000	Road segment intersections in Montgomery County (TIGER)
LB	57,000	Road segment intersections in Long Beach County (TIGER)
CP	62,000	Coordinates of various places in California (Sequoia 2000)
SU	100,000	Synthetic dataset with uniform distribution
SS	100,000	Synthetic dataset with skew distribution

Table 8.1. Description of datasets.

4.2 The Cost Model

Recall that the architecture we study here, assumes a network capable of performing multicasting. Also, we agree that when a server wants to transmit

Multiprocessor Query Processing

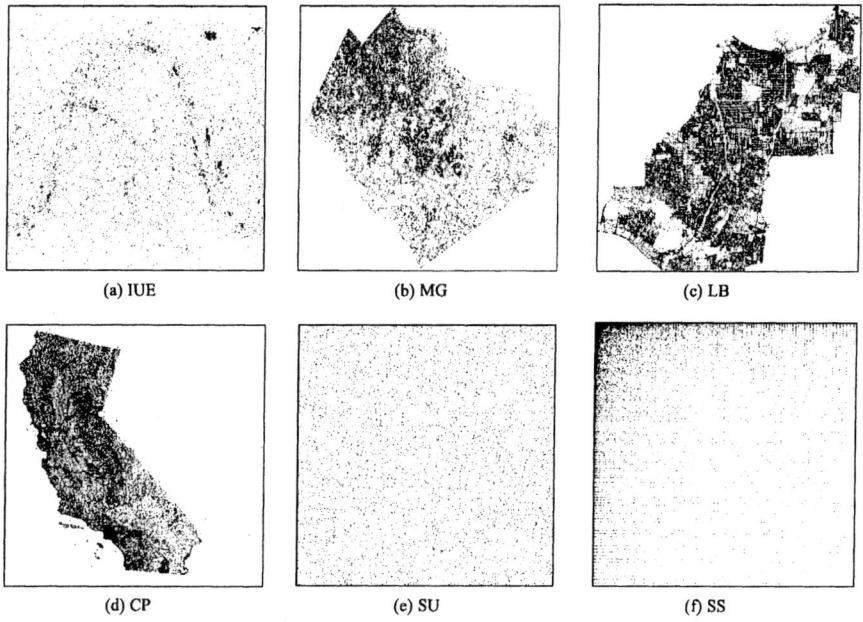

Figure 8.6. Graphical representation of datasets used for experimentation.

data and the network media is available (no other server is currently using it) then the server will send the data immediately.

In Figure 8.7 above, we present an example of how the response time of a query can be calculated. Assume that the primary server initiates a NN query, and that the qualifying servers are S_1, S_2 and S_3. Each one of the servers will perform some local computations and local I/O to process its portion of the answer. Also, each one of the activated servers must transmit the results back to the primary server. In time point A, the primary server has searched the upper tree levels. Immediately, transmits a packet to activate the relevant servers. In time point B, all servers have received the request, and they start the local processing phase which includes retrieving and inspecting the corresponding data pages. In time point C, server S_1 completes its local processing phase, and since the network media is free, it starts the transmission of the results to the primary server. Although server S_3 completes its processing at time point D, it can not transmit the data because the network media is occupied by S_1. Eventually, S_1 completes the transmission of the results and therefore S_3 may commence the data delivery. Finally, server S_2 starts the transmission at time point G and at time point H the whole process is completed. Therefore, the response time ranges from the beginning of processing, until time point H.

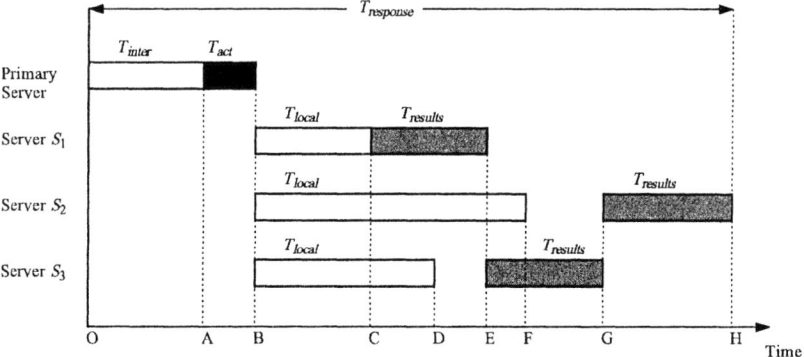

Figure 8.7. Calculation of the Response Time of a query.

We assume that a disk access of a page (either internal or leaf) has a cost of T_{page}=10ms. The total time T_{packet} to transmit a packet that contains b bytes equals:

$$T_{packet} = \frac{b}{NS} + T_{setup}$$

where NS is the network speed in bytes/second and T_{setup} is the time overhead required to prepare the packet and is set to 5ms. A similar approach has been followed in [62, 143].

4.3 Experimental Results

We conducted several series of experiments to test our proposed method and its behavior under different settings.

- In the first series of experiments, we compare the **P-NNF** and **BB-NNF** methods using all datasets. In Figure 8.8 we present the response times for the two methods using 10 secondary sites and high network speed (10Mbps). The value of k ranges between 1 and 1000.

- In the second series of experiments, we measure the number of frames transmitted over the network, the number of objects transmitted by each method and the time required to search the upper R-tree levels on the primary server. These results are illustrated in Figure 8.9 for the LB data set. Again, the value of k ranges between 1 and 1000.

Multiprocessor Query Processing

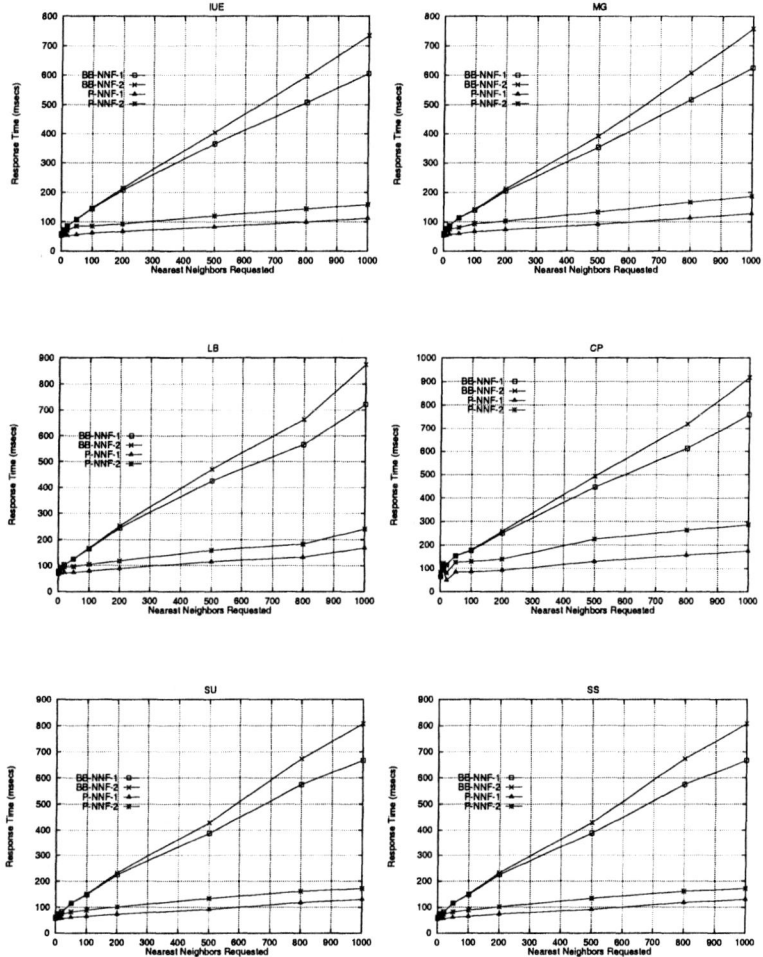

Figure 8.8. Response time (in msecs) vs. k (secondary sites=10, $NS_{eff} = 10Mbit/sec$).

- In the third series of experiments, we use sample values for the number k of nearest neighbors and test the changes in the response time with respect to the number of secondary sites (Figure 8.10) and the effective network speed (Table 8.2). The data set used is the LB. Three values of k are used, k_1=10, k_2=100 and k_3=200. In Figure 8.10, the number of secondary servers ranges between 1 and 30. In Table 8.2 the number of secondary servers is fixed at 10, whereas the effective network speed ranges between 10Kbit/sec to 10Mbit/sec.

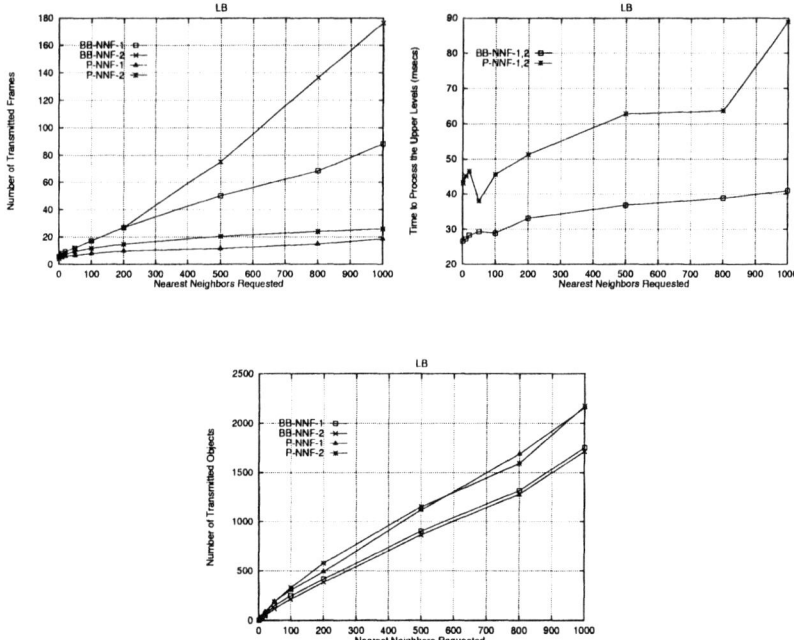

Figure 8.9. Number of transmitted frames, time to process the upper R-tree levels and number of transmitted objects, vs. k (secondary sites=10, $NS_{eff} = 10Mbit/sec$).

Since the behavior of the methods is similar for all datasets, in the second and third series of experiments we present results for the LB set only. All results are obtained after applying each nearest neighbor query 100 times and taking the average.

4.4 Interpretation of Results

The first observation derived from Figure 8.8 is that **P-NNF-1** method is superior to **BB-NNF-1**, **BB-NNF-2** and **P-NNF-2** methods in a parallel environment. The response time of a NN query is decreased drastically. In some cases, for small values of k (e.g. $k < 5$) the cost at the primary site may dominate and **BB-NNF** may be better. However, with the use of buffering, most of the internal tree nodes will be maintained in main memory, eliminating this problem. The general observation obtained from Figure 8.8 is that the performance gain of **P-NNF** over **BB-NNF** increases as k increases.

By inspecting Figure 8.9, we observe that **P-NNF-1** transmits the smallest number of network frames (packets). Therefore, the probability of collisions is reduced in comparison to all other methods. However, **P-NNF-1** transmits more objects than the other approaches. This is the price we pay to exploit

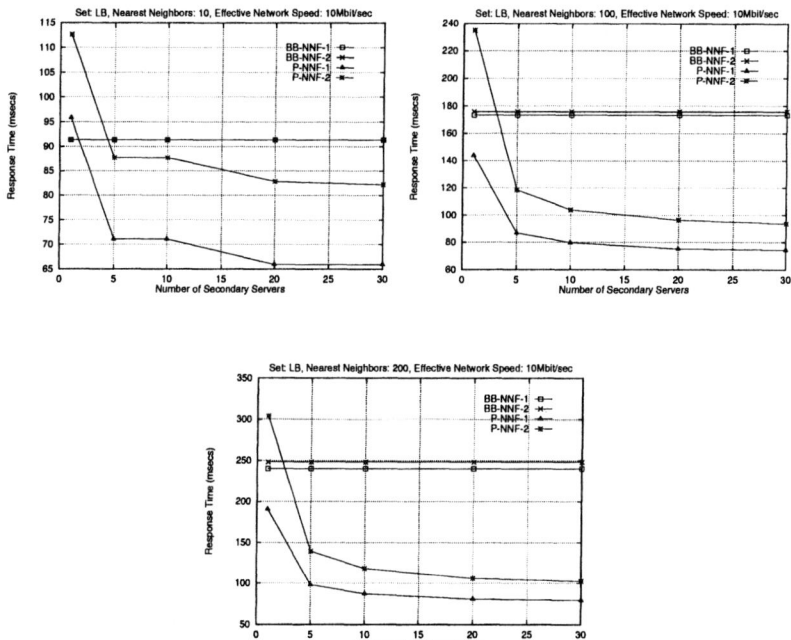

Figure 8.10. Response time (in msecs) vs. number of secondary servers.

parallelism. At the bottom of Figure 8.9 we observe that **BB-NNF-2** transmits the smallest number of objects, since each time a new data page is accessed and a server is activated, the currently best k distances are transmitted as well.

With respect to the overhead to search the upper R-tree levels, that are stored on the primary server, we can state that **BB-NNF** methods process fewer number of nodes than **P-NNF**. The increased number of nodes processed in **P-NNF** methods is due to the circular range query applied. Since the primary site stores only the upper R-tree levels, these could be maintained in main memory and therefore the processing cost would be very small.

In the **P-NNF** method, as the number of secondary sites increases, the response time decreases. However, the degree of parallelism is a function of the values of k and the number of secondary sites. On the other hand, the response time in **BB-NNF-1,2** methods remains constant since the method does not exploit any parallelism. These remarks are illustrated in Figure 8.10.

The network load has a very strong impact on the performance of both methods as shown in Table 8.2. In fact, under high network loads, the gain of **P-NNF** over **BB-NNF** decreases. This is an expected outcome, since the network usage time outperforms by factors the local processing time at each site and therefore, the benefits of parallel processing are no more existent. However, since fiber

NS_{eff} in Kbit/sec	BB-NNF-1	BB-NNF-2	P-NNF-1	P-NNF-2
	Nearest Neighbors: 10			
10000	91.35	91.37	67.25	84.27
1000	95.43	95.64	72.96	90.10
200	112.60	113.53	88.95	104.54
100	137.38	139.30	100.00	118.93
10	593.15	612.36	443.92	514.47
	Nearest Neighbors: 100			
10000	175.97	178.43	82.94	108.33
1000	199.58	224.90	100.69	130.31
200	273.97	387.72	179.02	220.18
100	404.69	649.52	297.99	373.64
10	2597.12	5103.60	2427.55	3043.70
	Nearest Neighbors: 200			
10000	226.63	234.12	80.56	110.31
1000	273.55	353.18	107.70	145.04
200	410.21	792.25	239.47	314.64
100	584.58	1355.55	408.39	543.78
10	3978.71	11974	3578.12	4398.77

Table 8.2. Response Time vs. network speed (Secondary sites=10, NN requested = 10, 100 and 200).

optics technology is becoming more and more available, reaching speeds of 1000Mbps, the use of **P-NNF** is recommended.

5. Summary

In this chapter, we study the performance of NN queries in multidisk multiprocessor architectures. We assume that data objects are stored in an R-tree and the whole structure is distributed over a number of servers, each with a single processor and a single disk attached. The basic motivation behind this work is the fact that the branch-and-bound algorithm of Roussopoulos et. al. [106] is strictly serial and therefore, cannot be applied directly in a parallel environment. We use statistical information to estimate the number of leaf accesses introduced due to the processing of a k-NN query and we use this estimation, in order to provide an efficient execution strategy. As long as the number of objects inserted or deleted is small, the statistical information need not be updated. The renewal of statistical data would be necessary after a large number of insertions/deletions.

Moreover, we present a modified algorithm to process NN queries in parallel, when statistical data are not available. Experimental results based on real-life and synthetic datasets show that the proposed **P-NNF** algorithms outperform the **BB-NNF** algorithms by factors. The efficiency measure is the query response time, which contains communication cost and local processing cost at each server. We test our method for light-loaded and heavy-loaded networks, different number of servers, different data populations and distributions and we observe that the response time is decreased drastically.

With respect to the generalization to higher dimensional spaces, the basic linearity observation stated in Subsection 8.2, may no longer hold, due to increased overlap between node MBRs. In this case, we need to estimate the number of data page accesses either using higher-order regression models, or accurate closed formed formulae.

Although we focused on packed R-trees, the method can equally well be applied in dynamic environments. In such an environment, packed R-trees are not recommended because the structure characteristics change rapidly due to insertions and deletions of data. Instead, another variant should be used (e.g. R*-tree [7], dynamic Hilbert R-tree [29]), that is better equipped to handle the dynamic behavior.

6. Further Reading

Other approaches for parallel query processing by using spatial access methods have been studied in [41], where the authors study data-parallel algorithms for spatial operations using data-parallel variants of the bucket PMR quadtree, R-tree, and R^+-tree. The algorithms are implemented using the scan model of parallel computation on a hypercube architecture.

Efficient algorithms for parallel intersection spatial join processing have been proposed in [17], whereas in [6, 116] efficient techniques have been reported for parallel similarity join processing.

Declustering and load-balancing for non-point objects are studied in [118], where the authors study several critical issues for parallelizing Geographical Information Systems. An important issue that is covered in this work, is the declustering of complex non-point objects.

Chapter 9

DISTRIBUTED QUERY PROCESSING

1. Introduction

In Chapter 8 we have focused on a parallel architecture composed of a network of workstations, where data are declustered amongst the available processors. In this chapter, we study NN query processing in a distributed database system. More specifically, we make no assumptions about the data declustering method, since each database is considered autonomous. However, we assume that each autonomous database is capable of answering NN queries in its local data, although different databases could exploit different algorithms and access methods.

Since no particular declustering scheme can be assumed, the algorithms studied in the pervious chapters can not be applied in this case. The system is composed of a primary server that operates as a coordinator for the m source databases. All systems are communicating via a network configuration (Figure 9.1).

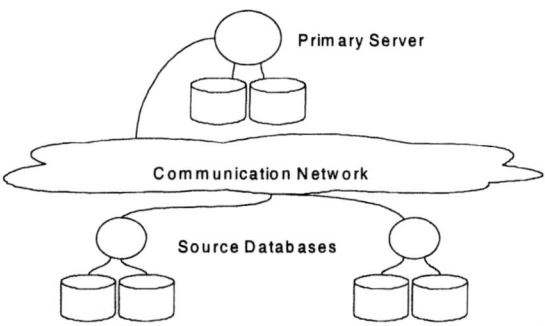

Figure 9.1. The abstract system architecture.

The primary server may be a data warehouse or simply a system that is responsible for controlling and supervising the source databases. We assume that query requests are initiated by a user's system and then submitted to the primary server for evaluation. Also, the query results are gathered from the source databases to the primary server and then are shipped back to the appropriate user's system. Despite the fact that we perform a distinction between primary and secondary sites, any secondary site could take responsibility of evaluating user queries. Each source database has complete control over the objects that it stores. Therefore, different access methods and optimization techniques may be utilized by the different databases.

Definition 9.1
Given a k-NN query Q, the response time for Q is defined as the time elapsed from query submission to query completion. □

The challenge is to determine an efficient method for NN query processing in a distributed system. Moreover, the number of parameters is quite large and in some cases trade-offs occur (e.g., the degree of parallelism vs. the number of transmitted objects). The problem we are going to deal with in the remainder of the chapter is stated as follows:

Problem Statement
Given a distributed multidimensional database and a k-NN query Q_k, find an efficient evaluation strategy, to minimize the response time of Q_k and to consume as few overall system resources as possible. □

In order to approach the problem from a theoretical point of view, several simplifying assumptions should be introduced, resulting in a more feasible and tractable analysis. The basic assumptions introduced are summarized below:

1 Although we do not require the source databases to be homogeneous, we will assume that the cost to answer a given query is the same, for all source databases.

2 We assume that the similarity metric between two multidimensional vectors is the Euclidean distance (L_2 metric), and every database respects this similarity measure.

3 The data are partitioned to the source databases in such a way that no replication exists. In other words, each object is stored in only one database.

4 If during processing we must retrieve L disk pages from a source database, the required time is $L \cdot T_p$, where T_p is the expected page access time [1].

The material of this chapter is based on [96] and is organized as follows. Section 2 studies different query processing strategies, whereas Section 3 discusses briefly the impact of derived data. Section 4 contains the performance evaluation which demonstrates the performance of the methods under different parameter values. Section 5 discusses several important issues, whereas Section 6 concludes.

2. Query Evaluation Strategies
2.1 Algorithms

Let a k-NN query, Q_k, be submitted for evaluation to the primary server. Our first approach is to examine the query evaluation when no derived data are available. In a following section, we discuss what kind of derived data are necessary to improve the efficiency in similarity query processing. We could define two extreme strategies to answer the query:

Concurrent Processing - CP: Submit the query to all m source databases and collect k objects from each one. Among the $m \cdot k$ objects, select the best k (those that are closer to the query object).

Selective Processing - SP: First activate one source database. Collect the best k answers. Send only the distances of these k objects to the next source database and collect another l objects, where $0 \leq l \leq k$. Continue until all source databases are visited and the best matches have been determined.

We note that the first method tries to maximize parallelism but retrieves too many objects ($m \cdot k$), whereas the second method, performs a more refined search, but no parallelism is exploited. Therefore, we define the next method, which is a combination of the two previous ones:

Two-Phase Processing - 2PP: First visit f source databases and collect $f \cdot k$ objects. Then, select the best k and send the k distances to the rest $m - f$ source databases. Finally, collect the answers and determine the final set of nearest neighbors.

Finally, we define a last method that performs an optimistic search, pretending that each source database will contribute with almost the same number of objects.

Probabilistic Processing - PRP: First request $k/m + 1$ objects from each source database. Then, formulate the current set of best matches, and if there are sources that are still relevant, visit them again and collect the final set of objects.

By requesting $k/m + 1$ objects from each database, we can reject a database if the $(k/m + 1)$-th distance from the query point is larger than the best k-th distance determined so far.

2.2 Theoretical Study

We proceed with some theoretical investigation, regarding the efficiency of the four query evaluation strategies. The results will give some insight with respect to the efficiency of each approach under different settings.

Symbol	Description	Value
m	number of source databases	5 - 30
N	total number of objects	100,000 - 10,000,000
N_j	number of objects in j-th source database	N/m
d	dimensionality of the vector space	2 - 20
S_n	size of a number in bytes	4
S_o	average size of an object in bytes	100 - 100,000
S_v	size of a d-dimensional vector in bytes	$d \cdot S_n$
S_p	size of a disk page in bytes	4K
S_{header}	size of a network packet header in bytes	24
S_{pmax}	size of a network packet in bytes (without header)	1500
T_p	page read time in seconds	0.01
k	number of nearest neighbors requested	1 - 500
C_j	contribution of j-th source database	
NC_j	net contribution of the j-th source database	
$R_j(k)$	query response time (in seconds) for strategy j	
NS	network speed in bytes per second	100,000 - 1,000,000
f	visited databases in step 1 of **2PP** algorithm	1

Table 9.1. Symbols, definitions and corresponding values.

Table 9.1 presents the basic symbols and the corresponding definitions that are extensively used throughout this chapter. With $R_j(k)$ we denote the average query response time in seconds, for strategy j to answer a k-NN query. The total processing cost comprises of three basic parts: CPU cost, I/O cost and communication cost. We expect that CPU cost will have a small impact on the performance comparison of the strategies and therefore, it is excluded from our theoretical study. However, CPU cost is included in our experimental study

Distributed Query Processing 131

presented in a subsequent section.

Definition 9.2
We call *contribution* C_j of the j-th source database, the number of objects processed and transmitted during the evaluation of a k-NN query. Obviously, $C_j \leq k$ for all j, where $1 \leq j \leq m$ and $\sum_{j=1}^{m} C_j \geq k$. □

Definition 9.3
We call *net contribution* NC_j of the j-th source database, the number of objects from the j-th database that participate in the answer set of a k-NN query. Obviously, $0 \leq NC_j \leq k$, for all j, where $1 \leq j \leq m$ and $\sum_{j=1}^{m} NC_j = k$. □

Note that the contribution of a source database depends on the visiting sequence. Evidently, the net contribution of a source database is independent of the visiting sequence and depends on the data placement and the query point location. Under the uniformity and independence assumption, we expect that the net contribution of each database equals k/m.

Definition 9.4
The local processing cost of a source database to process a k-NN query is defined as:

$$Cost_{db} = \left(INA(k) + \frac{S_o}{S_p} \cdot k\right) \cdot T_p \qquad (9.1)$$

where $INA(k)$ refer to the number of index node accesses for k nearest neighbors, which depends on the database population, the space dimensionality and the data structure used to store and manipulate the objects, T_p is the page read time, S_o is the average number of bytes per database object, S_p is the number of bytes per disk page and O is the number of objects that are accessed. We note that the first part of the above equation is due to the index search, whereas the second one is due to the access of the object detailed descriptions. □

Here we describe the derivation for the local processing cost in a source database. This cost is composed of two components: (i) the cost to search the index and (ii) the cost to access the objects. From [29] the average number of R-tree node accesses (INA) for a window query is given by the following equation:

$$INA(k) = \sum_{j=0}^{h-1} \frac{N}{C_{eff}^{h-j}} \cdot \prod_{i=1}^{d} \left(q_s + \left(\frac{C_{eff}^{h-j}}{N}\right)^{1/d}\right) \qquad (9.2)$$

where N is the number of objects, h is the tree height, d is the dataspace dimensionality, C_{eff} is the average node capacity, and q_s is the window size in each dimension. The space is normalized to the unit hypercube.

In order to exploit the previous formula, we assume that the objects are uniformly distributed in the address space. Under this assumption, if k denotes the number of objects contained in a query volume $Vol(Q)$, the following holds:

$$\frac{Vol(Q)}{Vol(Space)} = \frac{k}{N}$$

Therefore, if the query volume corresponds to a hyper-rectangle, the window size q_s equals:

$$q_s = \sqrt[d]{Vol(Q)} \Rightarrow q_s = \sqrt[d]{\frac{k}{N}}$$

Substituting the value of q_s in Equation (9.2), we obtain a formula to estimate the expected number of node accesses during the execution of a NN query asking for the k nearest neighbors.

$$INA(k) = \sum_{j=0}^{h-1} \frac{N}{C_{eff}^{h-j}} \cdot \prod_{i=1}^{d} \left(\sqrt[d]{\frac{k}{N}} + \left(\frac{C_{eff}^{h-j}}{N} \right)^{1/d} \right)$$

On the number of index node accesses we have to add the number of additional pages that need to be retrieved to fetch the objects from the disk. To read k objects each having a size of S_o bytes each, we need to read $\frac{S_o}{S_p} \cdot k$ disk pages. Since each access costs T_p seconds, the total local processing cost of answering a NN query in a source database equals:

$$Cost_{local} = \left(INA(k) + \frac{S_o}{S_p} \cdot k \right) \cdot T_p \qquad (9.3)$$

We would like to note that the above cost model does not include buffer management or boundary effects due to high dimensionality. In these cases, other models could have been used instead. However, we used Equation (9.2) because of its simplicity, and because it can be used to model non-uniform distributions [29].

Definition 9.5
The cost for transmitting B bytes using the communications network is defined as follows:

$$Cost_{trans}(B) = \frac{1}{NS} \cdot \left(B + \frac{B}{S_{pmax}} \cdot S_{header} \right) \qquad (9.4)$$

Distributed Query Processing

where NS is the network speed in bytes per second, S_{pmax} is the maximum capacity of a network packet, and S_{header} is the packet header size in bytes. □

Based on the assumptions and the definitions given, let us proceed with a comparative study among the four methods described in the previous paragraphs. For each strategy, an estimation of the query response time is presented, giving an indication of the query processing performance. In the sequel, we denote with $Cost_{act}$ the cost to activate a database, with $Cost_{db}$ the processing cost in each database, and with $Cost_{result}$ the cost to collect the results from a database. We assume that the network does not support multicasting. In a different case, the derived costs will be slightly different.

Concurrent Processing

A message comprising of the query vector and the number k of nearest neighbors requested is submitted from the primary server to all source databases, one at a time. This costs:

$$Cost_{act} = Cost_{trans}(S_v + S_n)$$

Since all source databases receive the query request almost at the same time, the local processing cost equals:

$$Cost_{db} = \left(INA(k) + \frac{S_o}{S_p} \cdot k\right) \cdot T_p$$

Finally, the primary server must collect k objects from each source database. Therefore:

$$Cost_{result} = Cost_{trans}(k \cdot (S_n + S_o))$$

Summing up all costs we get:

$$R_{CP}(k) = m \cdot Cost_{act} + Cost_{db} + m \cdot Cost_{result} \qquad (9.5)$$

Selective Processing

All source databases are activated by sending the query vector and the number k of nearest neighbors requested. This costs:

$$Cost_{act} = Cost_{trans}(S_v + S_n)$$

For each subsequent source database (except the first one) the primary server must transfer the current k best distances:

$$Cost_{act2} = Cost_{trans}(k \cdot S_n)$$

because we must send the k distances of the best objects obtained so far. Let each source database j process C_j objects. Then, the local processing cost equals:

$$Cost_{db} = \left(INA(k) + \frac{S_o}{S_p} \cdot C_j\right) \cdot T_p$$

The transmission of C_j objects from source database j to the primary server costs:

$$Cost_{result} = Cost_{trans}((S_o + S_n) \cdot C_j)$$

Summing up all costs we get:

$$R_{SP}(k) = m \cdot Cost_{act} + (m-1) \cdot Cost_{act2} + \sum_{j=1}^{m} Cost_{db} + \sum_{j=1}^{m} Cost_{result} \tag{9.6}$$

Two-Phase Processing

First, the f source databases are activated by sending the query vector and the number k of nearest neighbors requested. This costs:

$$Cost_{act} = Cost_{trans}(S_v + S_n)$$

Each of the f source databases will process k objects in parallel, costing:

$$Cost_{db1} = \left(INA(k) + \frac{S_o}{S_p} \cdot k\right) \cdot T_p$$

The transfer of k objects from each of the f source databases costs:

$$Cost_{result1} = Cost_{trans}(k \cdot (S_o + S_n))$$

The activation of the rest $m - f$ source databases requires the transfer of the current best k distances plus the query vector:

$$Cost_{act2} = Cost_{trans}(k \cdot S_n)$$

The $m - f$ source databases process C objects each. Therefore, the local processing cost is:

$$Cost_{db2} = \left(INA(k) + \frac{S_o}{S_p} \cdot C\right) \cdot T_p$$

The primary server must collect C objects from each source database (among the $m - f$ ones) and therefore:

$$Cost_{result2} = Cost_{trans}(C \cdot (S_o + S_n))$$

Distributed Query Processing

In conclusion, the total cost for this strategy is given by:

$$\begin{aligned} R_{2PP}(k) &= m \cdot Cost_{act} + Cost_{db1} + f \cdot Cost_{result1} + \\ &+ (m-f) \cdot Cost_{act2} + Cost_{db2} + \\ &+ (m-f) \cdot Cost_{result2} \end{aligned} \tag{9.7}$$

Probabilistic Processing

A message comprising of the query vector and the number $k/m + 1$ of nearest neighbors requested is submitted from the primary server to all source databases. This costs:

$$Cost_{act} = Cost_{trans}(S_v + S_n)$$

Since all source databases receive the query request almost at the same time, the local processing cost equals:

$$Cost_{db} = \left(INA(k/m + 1) + \frac{S_o}{S_p} \cdot (k/m + 1) \right) \cdot T_p$$

Subsequently, the primary server must collect $k/m+1$ objects from each source database. Therefore:

$$Cost_{result} = Cost_{trans}((k/m + 1) \cdot (S_n + S_o))$$

In the best case of **PRP** (**PRP**$_{best}$) no further processing is required. However, in a typical case (**PRP**$_{avg}$) let m' be the number of reactivated databases, where each one contributes with C_j objects. The reactivation cost per database equals the transmission cost of the best k distances determined so far:

$$Cost_{act2} = Cost_{trans}(k \cdot S_n)$$

Each of the reactivated databases will perform further processing to determine the best k matches. Therefore, the cost per database equals:

$$Cost_{db2} = \left(INA(k) + \frac{S_o}{S_p} \cdot C_j \right) \cdot T_p$$

Finally, each reactivated database will transmit C_j objects, with cost:

$$Cost_{result2} = Cost_{trans}((S_o + S_n) \cdot C_j)$$

Summing up we obtain:

$$\begin{aligned} R_{PRP}(k) &= m \cdot Cost_{act} + Cost_{db} + m \cdot Cost_{result} + \\ &+ m' \cdot Cost_{act2} + Cost_{db2} + m' \cdot Cost_{result2} \end{aligned} \tag{9.8}$$

It is evident that the performance of **CP** is quite predictable, since each source database processes and transmits exactly k objects. However, to predict the performance of **SP** and **2PP**, further analysis is required. We need the following lemmas to proceed.

Lemma 9.1
Assume that $NC_j = \frac{k}{m}$ for all $1 \leq j \leq m$. Then the following holds:

1. The first accessed database that will process and transmit k objects.
2. The n-th database (where $n < m$) that we access, will process and transmit $k - n \cdot \frac{k}{m}$ objects in the worst case and $\frac{k}{m}$ objects in the best case.
3. The last (m-th) visited database will process and transmit exactly $\frac{k}{m}$ objects.

Proof
We examine each case separately:

1. This is straightforward, since no precomputed distances exist before the access of the first source database.
2. We know that the net contribution of the j-th source database is $NC_j = k/m$. This means that k/m is the minimum number of objects that each source database will process and transmit. To prove the upper bound, let us assume that the currently accessed database, transmits $l > (k - (n-1) \cdot \frac{k}{m})$ objects. This means that we have found $l - (k - (n-1) \cdot \frac{k}{m})$ objects in this database that are closer to the query point than some objects among the $(n-1) \cdot k/m$. Moreover, this fact implies that the net contribution of one or more databases that were accessed previously is not k/m but lower, which contradicts our assumption that the net contribution of each source database is k/m. Therefore, the upper bound in the number of transmitted objects for the n-th accessed database is $k - (n-1) \cdot \frac{k}{m}$.
3. This is a special case of 2 above by setting $n = m$. □

Lemma 9.2
The average number of objects processed and transmitted by a source database for a k-NN query by **SP** is:
$$\overline{O_{SP}} = \left(\frac{m^2 + 5m - 2}{4m^2}\right) \cdot k$$

Proof
According to Lemma 9.1, the n-th visited database source database will process and transmit k/m objects at best and $k - (n-1) \cdot \frac{k}{m}$ object at worst. Therefore, on average we expect that $(k - (n-2) \cdot \frac{k}{m})/2$ objects will be processed and transmitted. Taking into consideration all source databases, we have that the average number of processed objects per source database equals:
$$\overline{O_{SP}} = \frac{k}{m} + \frac{1}{m} \cdot \sum_{n=2}^{m} \frac{k \cdot m - (n-2) \cdot k}{2m} \Rightarrow \overline{O_{SP}} = \frac{m^2 + 5m - 2}{4m^2} \cdot k$$

Lemma 9.3

The average number of objects processed and transmitted by a source database for a k-NN query by **2PP** is:

$$\overline{O_{2PP}} = \left(\frac{2mf + (m-f)(m-f+1)}{2m^2}\right) \cdot k$$

Proof

Each of the f first accessed source databases will process k objects, resulting in a total of $f \cdot k$ objects. The rest $m - f$ databases will process at least k/m objects and at most $k - f \cdot \frac{k}{m}$ objects and on average $(k - (f-1) \cdot \frac{k}{m})/2$ objects. Taking all source databases into consideration we get:

$$\overline{O_{2PP}} = \frac{f \cdot k + (m-f) \cdot \frac{m \cdot k - (f-1) \cdot k}{2m}}{m} \Rightarrow$$

$$\overline{O_{2PP}} = \left(\frac{2mf + (m-f)(m-f+1)}{2m^2}\right) \cdot k$$

Evidently, if each database contributes exactly k/m objects, the **PRP** method needs only one phase, since no database will be reactivated. However, in a more typical case, some of the databases will be reactivated and further objects will be processed and transmitted. In such a case, the expected number of objects that each reactivated database will process is given by the following lemma.

Lemma 9.4

The average number of objects processed and transmitted by a source database for a k-NN query by the second step of **PRP** is:

$$\overline{O_{PRP}} = \frac{k \cdot (m-1) - m}{2 \cdot m}$$

Proof

In the first step, each database has transmitted $k/m + 1$ objects. Therefore, at least $k/m + 1$ best matches have been determined. In the second step, each database will transmit at least 0 and at most $k - (k/m + 1)$ objects. Therefore, the average number of objects equals $\frac{k - (k/m + 1)}{2}$.

According to the above lemmas, the average execution time for each evaluation strategy is given by the following formulae:

$$R_{CP}(k) = m \cdot Cost_{trans}(S_v + S_n) + \left(INA(k) + \frac{S_o}{S_p} \cdot k\right) \cdot T_p +$$
$$+ \ m \cdot Cost_{trans}(k \cdot (S_n + S_o)) \tag{9.9}$$

$$R_{SP}(k) = m \cdot Cost_{trans}(S_v + S_n) + (m-1) \cdot Cost_{trans}(k \cdot S_n) +$$
$$+ \ m \cdot \left(INA(k) + \frac{S_o}{S_p} \cdot \overline{O_{SP}}\right) \cdot T_p +$$
$$+ \ m \cdot Cost_{trans}((S_o + S_n) \cdot \overline{O_{SP}}) \tag{9.10}$$

$$R_{2PP}(k) = m \cdot Cost_{trans}(S_v + S_n) + 2 \cdot \left(INA(k) + \frac{S_o}{S_p} \cdot \overline{O_{2PP}}\right) \cdot T_p +$$
$$+ \ m \cdot Cost_{trans}(\overline{O_{2PP}} \cdot (S_o + S_n)) +$$
$$+ \ (m - f) \cdot Cost_{trans}(k \cdot S_n) \tag{9.11}$$

$$R_{PRP}(k) = m \cdot Cost_{trans}(S_v + S_n) +$$
$$+ \ \left(INA(k/m + 1) + \frac{S_o}{S_p} \cdot (k/m + 1)\right) \cdot T_p$$
$$+ \ m \cdot Cost_{trans}((k/m + 1) \cdot (S_n + S_o)) +$$
$$+ \ (m/2) \cdot Cost_{trans}(S_n \cdot k) +$$
$$+ \ \left(INA(k) + \frac{S_o}{S_p} \cdot \overline{O_{PRP}}\right) \cdot T_p +$$
$$+ \ (m/2) \cdot Cost_{trans}(\overline{O_{PRP}} \cdot (S_o + S_n)) \tag{9.12}$$

The scenario assumed in the above analysis (scenario A) is that the detailed object description is transmitted in addition to the distance from the query point. This is useful when the user requires the first answers to be available as quickly as possible, even if they do not correspond to the real nearest neighbors. As long as the size of each object is small (e.g., 100 bytes), there is relatively little overhead for processing and transmitting this extra information. On the other hand, for larger object sizes and large numbers of requested neighbors, this cost becomes very significant and may dominate with respect to the total response time. Therefore, another scenario (scenario B) that could be followed, is to first determine the object IDs and the distances to the query point, and then to reactivate the relevant databases to fetch the detailed description of only the best matches. Evidently, the cost for this last action is the same for every strategy. We do not present the equations for the second scenario, since are simpler versions of Equations (9.9) to (9.12). However, in the analytical and experimental evaluation we demonstrate both cases.

Equations (9.9) to (9.12) give the expected execution time for each strategy when the system is lightly loaded, and therefore the waiting time is negligible. The behavior of the methods under a system load is studied using an experimental evaluation (see Section 5).

2.3 Analytical Comparison

Summarizing the theoretical analysis, in this subsection we present a comparative study regarding the efficiency of the four strategies. We present some results, with respect to the formulae of the previous subsection, to study the behavior of the methods under different parameter values. The parameters modified and the corresponding values are summarized in Table 9.1. We note that these results correspond to the execution of a single query, which means that the impact of concurrent users is not taken into account.

In Figure 9.2 the four query evaluation methods are compared, based on the analytic results. This figure includes the results for the case where the object detailed descriptions are processed and transmitted. Evidently, the **PRP**$_{best}$ method outperforms by factors the other candidates. The response time of all methods is increased by increasing the number of nearest neighbors (see Figure 9.2(a)). **CP** is most affected by this increase, since every database processes and transmits k objects. Although **SP** transmits the smaller number of objects, the price paid is that no parallelism is exploited, and the response time is increased.

By increasing the number of dimensions, the processing cost in each database increases also. For large space dimensionalities (e.g., above 20) the cost to search the index becomes significant. In Figure 9.2(b) it is observed that methods **2PP** and **PRP**$_{avg}$ tend to converge, and the same is observed for the methods **CP** and **PRP**$_{best}$. For smaller dimensionalities (e.g. < 10) the **PRP** methods show clearly the best performance.

The impact of the effective network speed on the performance of the methods is illustrated in Figure 9.2(c). For small effective network speed (large network traffic), the **CP** shows the worst performance, since it transmits more objects than the other methods, and therefore the network becomes the bottleneck.

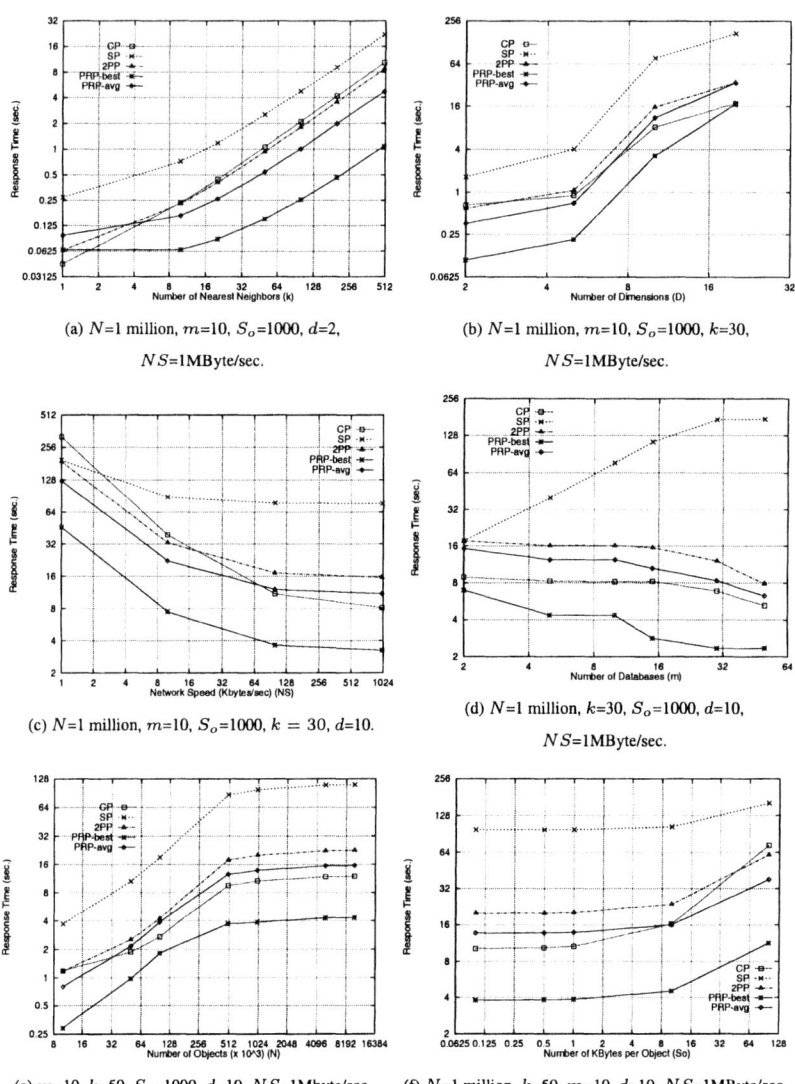

(a) $N=1$ million, $m=10$, $S_o=1000$, $d=2$, $NS=1$MByte/sec.

(b) $N=1$ million, $m=10$, $S_o=1000$, $k=30$, $NS=1$MByte/sec.

(c) $N=1$ million, $m=10$, $S_o=1000$, $k=30$, $d=10$.

(d) $N=1$ million, $k=30$, $S_o=1000$, $d=10$, $NS=1$MByte/sec.

(e) $m=10$, $k=50$, $S_o=1000$, $d=10$, $NS=1$Mbyte/sec.

(f) $N=1$ million, $k=50$, $m=10$, $d=10$, $NS=1$MByte/sec.

Figure 9.2. Performance of methods for scenario A (logarithmic scales).

Distributed Query Processing

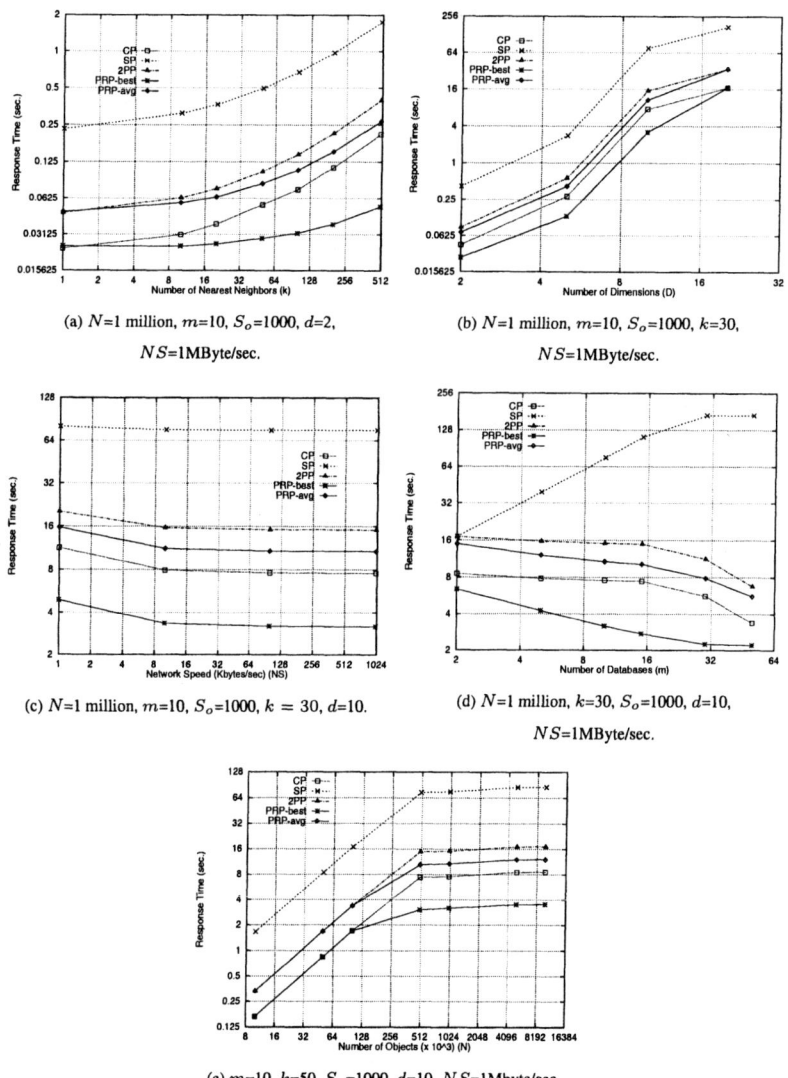

(a) $N=1$ million, $m=10$, $S_o=1000$, $d=2$, $NS=1$MByte/sec.

(b) $N=1$ million, $m=10$, $S_o=1000$, $k=30$, $NS=1$MByte/sec.

(c) $N=1$ million, $m=10$, $S_o=1000$, $k=30$, $d=10$.

(d) $N=1$ million, $k=30$, $S_o=1000$, $d=10$, $NS=1$MByte/sec.

(e) $m=10$, $k=50$, $S_o=1000$, $d=10$, $NS=1$Mbyte/sec.

Figure 9.3. Performance of methods for scenario B (logarithmic scales).

An interesting observation (see Figure 9.2(d)) is that the performance of **SP** is affected in a negative manner by increasing the number of databases, whereas the response time of the other methods is reduced. The cause for this behavior is that **SP** does not exploit intraquery parallelism.

The increase in the number of objects is depicted in Figure 9.2(e). Evidently, all methods are affected significantly. Finally, in Figure 9.2(f), the response time with respect to the object size is illustrated. The impact on object size growth is stronger for **CP**, since it processes and transmits more objects than the other methods.

In Figure 9.3 we illustrate the performance of the methods for the case where the detailed object description is not transmitted. It is observed that the results are not modified drastically with respect to the results in Figure 9.2.

The results presented in Figures 9.2 and 9.3 correspond to a single user system, with no other interference. In a general case however, many users are posing queries to the database, resulting in network traffic and competition for the CPU in each database. For example, although the **SP** method does not support intraquery parallelism, supports interquery parallelism, because it is possible to access all m databases for m different queries. On the other hand, we expect a large performance degradation for **CP** method, since for large number of concurrent users queues will grow larger in disks, CPU and the network. In the next section we examine the impact of concurrent users, giving experimental results on a real implementation of the query evaluation strategies over a network of workstations.

3. The Impact of Derived Data

In the previous section, we discussed evaluation strategies assuming that no derived data are available in the primary server. Therefore, all m source databases need to be visited to determine the best k matches to a given query object. However, in real applications, the presence of derived data is very important to avoid searching large dataspace portions without a chance to retrieve relevant objects. Moreover, we may avoid visiting a particular source database, if we are absolutely sure that no relevant objects can be found, reducing network contention and saving overall system resources. Several types of derived data can be useful, ranging from simple numerical values (e.g., the number of objects in the database) to more sophisticated ones and difficult to obtain (e.g., an exact description of the object distribution). We focus on derived data information that represent Minimum Bounding Boxes (MBB) of a set of objects. In other words, some descriptors are used to group objects in sets, e.g., two MBBs enclosing two different sets of objects.

In order to be able to discard quickly data space portions not related to the answer set, we require the presence of a set of MBBs stored in the primary server. For each source database j, the primary server maintains a number of MBBs.

Distributed Query Processing

The smaller the overlap of these MBBs the better the discrimination during query processing. Also, a large number of MBBs helps the discrimination process.

To illustrate the use of MBBs for discrimination among objects, we present a few examples in Figure 9.4. In Figure 9.4(a) two MBBs are shown, each holding five points in the 2-d space. Assume that the three nearest neighbors with respect to point P are required. Let the circle enclose the best matches determined so far, namely, the points 1, 2 and 3 of MBB1. Then we can safely avoid the search in MBB2, since there is no intersection with the circle.

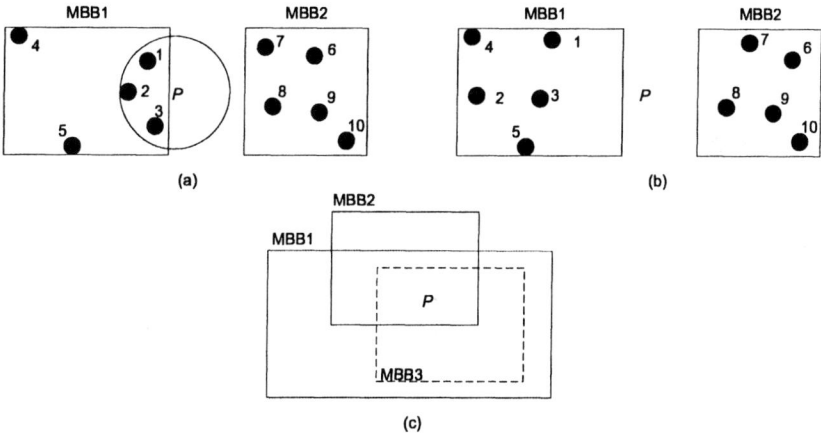

Figure 9.4. (a) Use of two MBBs for discrimination, (b) The nearest neighbor of P is not in MBB1, (c) A query point P enclosed by many MBBs.

Consider now a query point and a number of MBBs. The question posed is which MBB are we going to visit first and how can we safely prune any dataspace portions that are not promising. The order that we access the MBBs (and consequently the source databases), has a major impact on the efficiency of a query processing strategy, since it is highly correlated to the number of transmitted objects. The following lemma (which is easily generalized for an arbitrary number of source databases) shows why a "good" visiting order of the source databases is necessary and also explains what "good" means.

Lemma 9.5
Assume we have only two source databases SDB_1 and SDB_2 with net contributions NC_1 and NC_2 respectively, for a specific k–NN query. Assume further, without loss of generality, that $NC_1 \leq NC_2$. Then, the sum of contributions, $C_1 + C_2$, is maximized if the source databases are accessed in increasing net contribution order (i.e. SDB_1 first and SDB_2 second), and is minimized

if they are accessed in decreasing net contribution order (i.e. SDB_2 first and SDB_1 second).

Proof
Consider that we first visit SDB_1 and then SDB_2. The first database will contribute k objects and the second $NC_2 = k - NC_1$ objects (according to Lemma 9.1). This results in a total of $k + NC_2$ objects. Now, assume that we first access SDB_2 which will process k objects, and then SDB_1 which will process $NC_1 = k - NC_2$ objects. The total number of objects is $k + NC_1$. Evidently, $k + NC_1 \leq k + NC_2$ and this completes the proof. □

An approach used in [106] is to visit the MBBs according to the $MINDIST$ distance. The $MINDIST(P, R)$ distance is defined as the minimum distance between a query point P and an MBB R. Therefore, a sorted list of MBBs with respect to the query point is formulated and then we investigate each MBB, following the order. There are two main drawbacks with this approach, illustrated in Figure 9.4:

1 The fact that the query point P is closer to MBB R does not provide any guarantee that also the nearest neighbor(s) of P will be found in R (Figure 9.4(b)).

2 By definition, if a query point P falls inside an MBB R, then it hold that $MINDIST(P, R) = 0$. Therefore, in the case where P falls inside many MBBs $R_1, ..., R_n$, we are forced to select an MBB randomly, or apply another heuristic in order to resolve ties (Figure 9.4(c)).

Despite the above drawbacks of the $MINDIST$ approach, the method is simple and easily implemented. In a separate section we discuss further improvement that requires additional information. In the following lines, the query evaluation strategies are presented taking into account the derived data information.

CP
1. Determine the relevant source databases from derived data.
2. Send the query to the relevant databases.
3. Collect all answers.
4. Determine the best k matches.

SP
1. Determine the relevant source databases from derived data.
2. Using the $MINDIST$ metric, find the best source database to access.
3. Send the currently best distances to the database.
4. Collect answers.

5. Discard any source databases that do not require access.
6. If there is no database to access then STOP else GOTO 2.

2PP
1. Determine the relevant source databases from derived data.
2. Using the $MINDIST$ metric, find the best f databases to access.
3. Collect answers from the f databases.
4. Determine the currently best distances.
5. Discard any source databases that do not require access.
6. If there is no database to access then STOP.
7. Assume that s databases require access currently.
8. Access the s databases and collect the new answers.
9. Determine the best k matches.

PRP
1. Determine the relevant source databases from derived data.
2. Send the query to the r relevant databases, and collect $k/r + 1$ objects from each one.
3. Determine the current set of nearest neighbors.
4. Reactivate some of the databases if needed.
5. Determine the best k matches.

In all methods, we need first to determine the relevant source databases, and to discard any databases that is impossible to contribute to the answer set. This is performed by means of the $MAXDIST$ metric. The $MAXDIST$ between a point and an MBB is defined as the distance from the point to the furthest MBB vertex. The following lemma explains:

Lemma 9.6
Assume we have a set $\mathcal{M}_j$ of MBBs for each source database j. Let M_{ji}^n denote the number of objects that the MBB M_{ji} encloses. For simplicity let M_{ji}^n be equal for all j and i. We denote by R the distance between the query point P and the $\lceil k/M_{ji}^n \rceil$-th MBB with respect to the $MAXDIST$ metric, where k is the number of nearest neighbors requested. Then, all objects that participate in the answer set of nearest neighbors lie inside the circle with center P and radius R.

Proof
The circle C contains at least k objects, since we select for the circle radius the $MAXDIST$ to the $\lceil k/M_{ji}^n \rceil$-th MBB. If there is no other object inside the circle, then the k found so far are the best k matches. Any other object which

is closer to the query point than any of the k objects above, must lie inside the circle necessarily. □

4. Performance Evaluation
4.1 Preliminaries

The performance evaluation of the processing strategies were carried out on a cluster of five Silicon Graphics workstations, comprising the source databases. We used a SUN Sparcstation-4 for the primary server. The workstations were interconnected via a 10Mbit/sec Ethernet. Two types of processes were defined: 1) a client process running on the primary server and 2) a server process running on each source database. The responsibility of the client process is to pose queries to the source databases, whereas the responsibility of a server process is to serve the queries that are directed to the corresponding source database. The programs were coded in the C programming language under UNIX and the interprocess communication was based on the TCP/IP stream sockets programming interface [126].

We assume that each source database maintains an R-tree index for object storage and manipulation. Other data structures could have been used equally well. We generated random points in the 2-d, 3-d, 5-d and 10-d spaces. We can distinguish two ways to partition the objects to the source databases. In the first one, random assignment of objects to databases is used. In this approach, almost all source databases must be accessed to answer a similarity query. In the second one, each database is responsible for a small dataspace portion. In this approach, few databases must be accessed during query processing. Experiments have been conducted for the first case only, for brevity.

In order to study the performance of the methods under system load, we assume that users are posing queries concurrently to the primary server. Also, several values of the number of nearest neighbors requested were used and different object sizes. For each experiment the average response time per similarity query was calculated. Each user poses ten queries in total, and the queries are executed one-by-one.

4.2 Cost Model Evaluation

In a previous section a cost model has been derived for each query processing method. In order for these cost models to be useful, they should accurately predict the performance in real situations. Therefore, we start the experimental evaluation of the methods by first comparing the analytical formulae to the actual running time of each method.

In Figure 9.5 the theoretical and measured response time for queries are depicted for each method. The parameters used for the evaluation are summarized below: N=100,000, NS=1 MByte/sec, m=5, d=2, S_o=1000 bytes, f=1. The

Distributed Query Processing

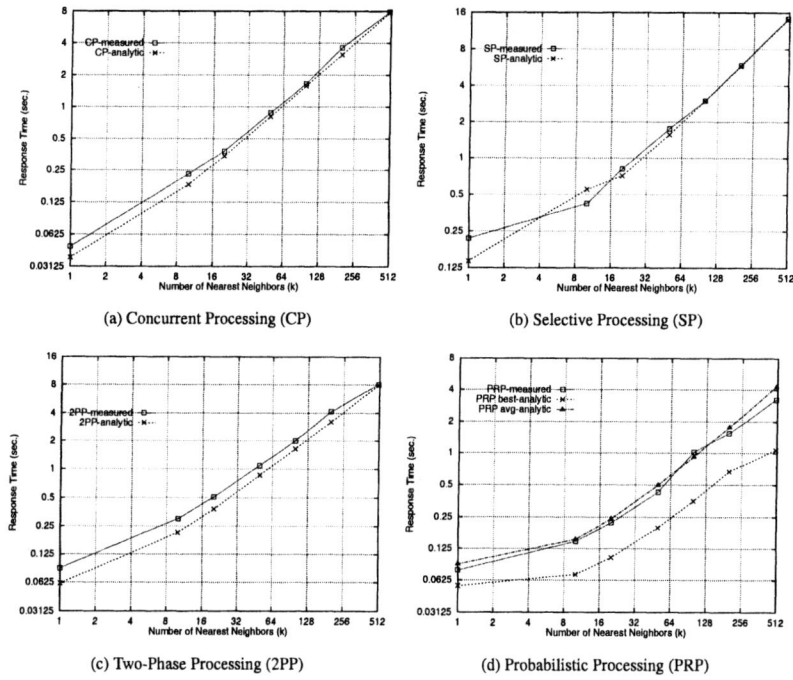

Figure 9.5. Cost model evaluation (logarithmic scales).

graphs are plotted in logarithmic scales so that the differences are clearer. It is evident that the cost models are quite accurate, since the maximum relative error is around 20%, whereas the average relative error is around 10%.

Therefore, the cost model can be used to accurately predict the performance of a query evaluation method. This enables to use the formulae for query optimization purposes or for selecting the appropriate method to answer a query according to the parameter values. More specifically, if one of the critical parameters (e.g., the effective network speed) changes, then by consulting the formulae the best method for the current settings can be selected. This gives the flexibility to the query execution engine to select the evaluation method that is expected to give the most promising results.

4.3 Experimental Results

In this subsection we illustrate representative results with respect to the real performance of the query evaluation strategies. Figure 9.6 illustrates the results when the detailed objects' description is processed and transmitted by the databases, whereas in Figure 9.7 these costs are not included. All graphs

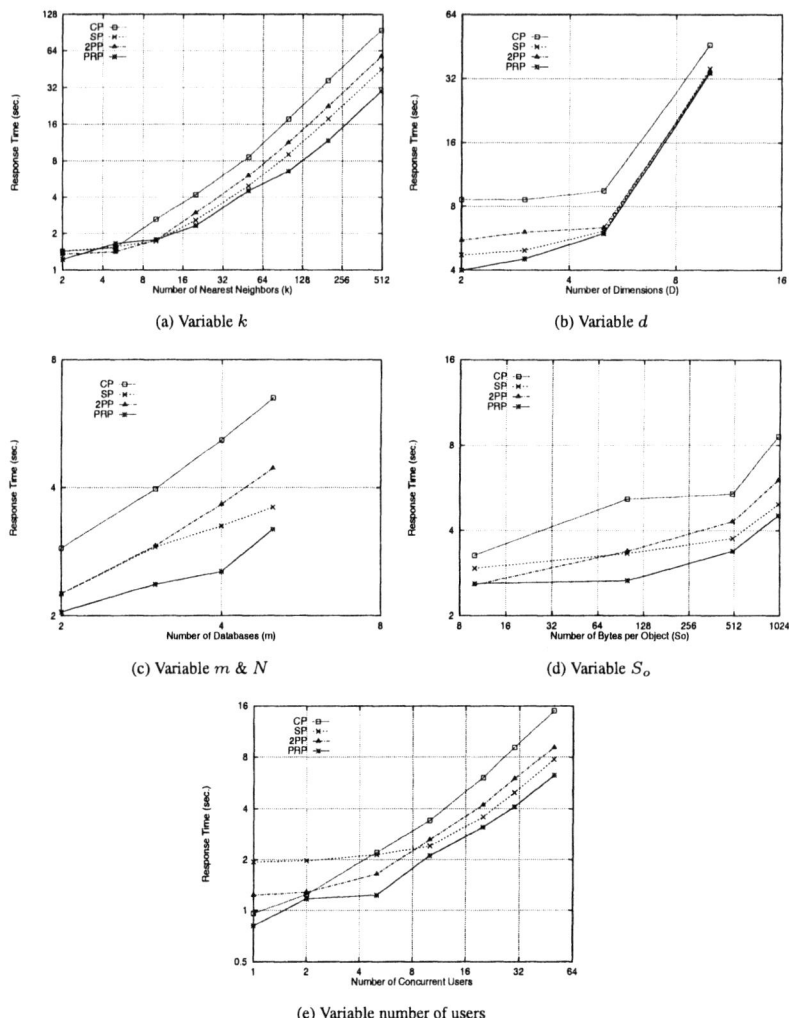

Figure 9.6. Measured response time for scenario A (logarithmic scales).

are plotted in logarithmic scales. In order to investigate the performance of the methods under system load, we assume that users are posing queries concurrently. Each user submits queries to the primary server one-by-one. The response time illustrated in the graphs is the average response time per query, calculated over all users. We note that the cost includes CPU time, since for large number of users we expect this cost to be significant, because of waiting time.

Distributed Query Processing

In Figure 9.6(a) we depict the response time with respect to the number of nearest neighbors k. For this experiment we used the following parameter values: N=250,000, d=3, m=5, S_o=1000, and f=1. Each database holds 50,000 objects. There are 30 users posing queries concurrently. For a small number of k (e.g., 2,3), **CP** performs quite well. However, when k increases, the performance of **CP** degrades. The reason is that **CP** demands k objects from each activated database, resulting in high resource consumption in the CPU, the disk, and the network. An interesting observation is that although **SP** does not exploit intraquery parallelism, its performance is very good in a multiuser system. However, **PRP** shows the best performance.

Figure 9.6(b) illustrates the method performance for different number of dimensions. Each database holds 50,000 objects. The remaining parameters have as follows: k=50, m=5, S_o=1000, and f=1. There are 30 concurrent users posing queries. Evidently, all methods are affected drastically by increasing the space dimensionality. The reason is that CPU and disk costs are higher, due to the increased index processing cost in each database.

Figure 9.6(c) illustrates the method performance for different number of databases, and different number of objects. Each database holds 50,000 objects. The remaining parameters have as follows: k=50, d=10, S_o=1000, and f=1. There are 30 concurrent users posing queries. **PRP** demonstrates the best performance, whereas the performance of **CP** degrades. By increasing the number of databases, more network traffic is anticipated, since **CP** requests k objects from each database. Also, **SP** and **2PP** have similar performance.

The impact of the object size is illustrated in Figure 9.6(d). This graph was produced using N=250,000, k=50, d=10, f=1 and assuming that there are 30 users posing queries. Evidently **CP** is affected more, and we expect higher degradation for larger number of bytes per object. Again **PRP** and **SP** demonstrate similar performance, and **PRP** performs the best.

The impact of the number of concurrent users is depicted in Figure 9.6(e). Again, N=250,000, k=50, d=3, S_o=1000, and f=1. When the number of users is relatively small (e.g., <10), the performance of **SP** degrades. This behavior is explained by taking into account that **SP** does not exploit intraquery parallelism. Therefore, the CPU and disk costs in each database are added, resulting in performance degradation. **CP**, **2PP** and **PRP** show similar performance. For a large number of concurrent users, **CP** is affected in a negative manner, because of bottlenecks. The other methods demonstrate similar performance, with **PRP** being the most efficient method.

In Figure 9.7 we illustrate the performance of the methods for scenario B, where the detailed object description is not transmitted by the databases before the k best matches have been determined. It is interesting to note that in most cases **SP** does not perform well, unlike scenario A. The network traffic is reduced, and this is in favor for **CP**, **2PP** and **PRP**. The only exception occurs

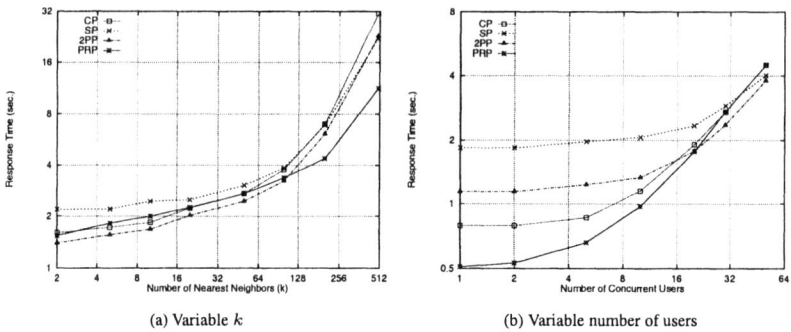

Figure 9.7. Measured response time for scenario B (logarithmic scales).

for a large number of concurrent users (e.g.,50) where the performance of the methods tends to converge (see Figure 9.7(b)).

5. Discussion

In this section we discuss some issues that are of major importance and can be considered for improvements in the future:

- Care should be taken when designing the derived data. If the number of derived data objects is large, then the primary server may become a bottleneck due to the increased CPU time required to process them. The reason is that a large number of MBBs helps in better pruning during query processing but, on the other hand, increases the required processing time. Therefore, it would be useful to maintain a separate data structure for the derived data to speed up processing.

- The generation of the derived data is very important. If the objects are manipulated by the source databases using a data structure based on Minimum Bounding Boxes (e.g., R-trees, R^+-trees) then we can use an intermediate tree level to extract the MBBs needed by the primary server (see for example [58]). On the other hand, if the corresponding data structures are not MBB based, then the MBBs should be generated artificially.

- As explained in Section 4, the $MINDIST$ approach can lead to a not that efficient access order of the source databases. A number of additional reference points may help in better ordering of the source databases. For example, a reference point may be the center of a cluster of objects. Therefore, if a specific cluster center is closer to the query point than other cluster centers, we have a good chance that this particular cluster will contribute the most to the final answer set of nearest neighbors. The point here is that additional computation is required to extract the clustering information from the source databases and, also, to exploit this information during query processing. The fact that cluster centers will improve processing performance still needs to be justified through experimental evaluation.

- A major issue that affects the performance of all methods is the object placement to databases. Since we allow each database to have separate and complete control over its stored objects, insertions and deletions of objects will create high overlaps among the dataspaces of the databases. This effect results in accessing many source databases for a single query. On the other hand, if we force centralized control (i.e. a single site is responsible for insertions/deletions/reorganizations), then it is still an open problem to derive optimal data placement techniques for similarity query processing.

6. Summary

We have examined the problem of multidimensional similarity query processing in a distributed system. The problem is well studied for the centralized case, and a number of very efficient methods have been proposed. However, in a distributed database system we have to take into consideration the communication overhead, in addition to the CPU and I/O cost, especially when the size of each object is not negligible. Four query evaluation strategies were developed and studied analytically and experimentally. The efficiency of each method depends heavily on several parameters such as the number of available source databases, the object placement in the databases, the object volume, the space dimensionality, the communication speed, the number of nearest neighbors requested, and the number of users issuing queries concurrently.

Each of the studied query evaluation strategies has its advantages and disadvantages, and the performance varies according to the parameters. Generally, methods **2PP** and **PRP** are the most robust, whereas **CP** and **SP** are sensitive to the multiprogramming degree and the database processing cost. However, they can be used in special cases. The developed cost model can be used to predict the performance of a query evaluation method.

7. Further Reading

In several cases, each database uses its own similarity function and therefore specialized processing techniques are required. An interesting approach that applies when there are multiple systems (databases) with different similarity measures is proposed in [27, 105]. The proposed techniques can be applied either to a distributed system or to a centralized one which is composed of different modules with different similarity models.

Recently, there is a major interest in the research community for providing efficient similarity query processing for the World Wide Web. For example, in

[76] a relational algebra is proposed for web and multimedia data, whereas in [39] several similarity-based strategies are studied. With the exploding growth of the WWW, such techniques will be valuable towards effective and efficient web search.

Epilogue

The last few decades, research in spatial and high-dimensional databases has been very significant, and some very efficient query processing techniques have been proposed. These efficient techniques are usually supported by sophisticated access methods, enabling the indexing of the underlying dataset and the pruning of irrelevant database parts. Applications that require the manipulation of multidimensional datasets range from simple geographic applications (e.g., GIS) to large multimedia databases. Although the data characteristics may be different in each application, the proposed query processing techniques are mainly based on the filter-refinement processing methodology. The target is, during processing, to quickly discard irrelevant database parts in the filter step, and perform a detailed processing of the candidate set.in the refinement step. The filter step is supported by indexing schemes, whereas the refinement step is performed by considering the dataset details.

Several indexing schemes have been proposed to handle multidimensional datasets. Amongst these schemes, the R-tree family is the most influential. Indeed, R-tree variations have been successfully applied to diverse research fields ranging from spatial and spatiotemporal databases, to data mining.and OLAP applications. The simplicity of the structure and the resemblance to the ubiquitous B-tree are two of the main motivations for its use in research prototypes and commercial systems. Efficient algorithms for range, nearest neighbor and join queries for the R-tree have been proposed and evaluated analytically and experimentally.

NN queries are very significant in spatial and multimedia applications. They allow the determination of the k closest objects with respect to a query object. The "closeness" is determined by means of a distance measure (e.g. Euclidean). This problem has been addressed before in the context of computational geometry, and recently a lot of research work has been performed from the database point of view. A naive way to process a k-NN query is to use repetitive range queries, by adjusting the search distance. Although simple, this approach can lead to significant performance degradation because either too few or too many objects are returned. In order to solve this problem, efficient NN algorithms have been proposed, which they assume the existence of an efficient indexing scheme. Specialized methods for high-dimensional datasets have also been proposed. The latter methods are extremely useful in multimedia applications, where objects are transformed to a high-dimensional space, by using selected features.

The research efforts in spatial databases paved the way for efficient query processing in spatiotemporal databases, where time plays a critical role. Several specialized access methods have been proposed to support time in data representation and user queries. In a database of moving objects, it is important to track object movement to either perform trajectory analysis, or to predict the future location of the moving objects. Query processing in such a case becomes very difficult, because the continuous object movement must be handled carefully.

In order to support spatial or multimedia query optimization, several cost models have been proposed that estimate the cost of a k-NN query. Cost estimation is very important, because it can be used during query optimization to determine an efficient query execution plan. Although the derivation of cost estimations for range queries are relatively easy, this is not true in the case of NN queries. The main problem is the estimation of the distance from the query point to its k-th nearest neighbor.

The performance of a database system can be improved either by exploiting more efficient algorithms and access methods, or by increasing the processing power of the computer system. An example of the latter case is the exploitation of multiple resources (disks, processors or both) towards more efficient data processing. Research in parallel and distributed database systems studies efficient data storage and processing techniques, aiming at the decrease of query response time.

In this book, we touched all the aforementioned research issues, by studying selected problems in NN search, by assuming a database point of view. However, the recent literature in NN search studies several interesting research directions in the area, such as:

- the development of efficient access methods and algorithms for NN query processing in *data streams*,

- the study of more efficient methods for NN search in location-aware services,

- the application of NN search in clustering algorithms for data mining,

- the development of accurate cost models for cost estimation of complex queries involving nearest neighbors (e.g., closest-pair queries),

- the study of more efficient techniques for querying moving objects on fixed spatial networks, where the objects' movement is constraint by an underlying network,
- the application of NN search to other disciplines like similarity search in biological data, similarity search in web usage data and similarity of moving-object trajectories.

References

[1] D.J. Abel, B.C. Ooi, K.-L. Tan, R. Power and J.X. Yu: "Spatial Join Strategies in Distributed Spatial DBMS", *Proceedings of the 4th International Symposium in Spatial Databases (SSD'95)*, pp.348-367, Portland, ME, 1995.

[2] N. R. Adam and A. Gangapadhyay: "*Database Issues in Geographical Information Systems*", Kluwer Academic Publishers, 1997.

[3] D.W. Adler: "IBM DB2 Spatial Extender - Spatial Data within the DBMS", *Proceedings of the 27th International Conference on Very Large Databases (VLDB'01)*, pp.687-690, Roma, Italy, 2001.

[4] P.K. Agarwal, L. Arge and J. Erickson: "Indexing Moving Points", *Proceedings of the 19th ACM SIGACT-SIGMOD-SIGART Symposium on Principles of Database Systems (PODS'00)*, pp.175-186, Dallas, TX, 2000.

[5] R. Agrawal, C. Faloutsos, and A. Swami: "Efficient Similarity Search in Sequence Databases", *Proceedings of the 4th International Conference on Foundations of Data Organization and Algorithms (FODO'93)*, pp.69-84, Evanston, IL, 1993.

[6] K. Alsabti, S. Ranka and V. Singh: "An Efficient Parallel Algorithm for High Dimensional Similarity Join", *Proceedings of the 11th International Parallel Processing Symposium*, pp.556-560, Orlando, FL, 1998.

[7] N. Beckmann, H.P. Kriegel and B. Seeger: "The R*-tree: an Efficient and Robust Method for Points and Rectangles", *Proceedings of the ACM International Conference on Management of Data (SIGMOD'90)*, pp.322-331, Atlantic City, NJ, 1990.

[8] A. Belussi, E. Bertino and B. Catania: "Using Spatial Data Access Structures for Filtering Nearest Neighbor Queries", *Data and Knowledge Engineering*, Vol.40, No.1, pp.1-31, 2002.

[9] A. Belussi and C. Faloutsos: "Estimating the Selectivity of Spatial Queries Using the 'Correlation' Fractal Dimension", *Proceedings of the 21st International Conference on Very Large Databases (VLDB'95)*, pp.299-310, Zurich, Switzerland, 1995.

[10] R. Benetis, C.S. Jensen, G. Karciauskas and S. Saltenis: "Nearest Neighbor and Reverse Nearest Neighbor Queries for Moving Objects", *Proceedings of the 6th International*

Database Engineering and Applications Symposium (IDEAS'02), pp.44-53, Edmonton, Canada, 2002.

[11] S. Berchtold, C. Boehm, B. Braunmueller, D. A. Keim and H.-P. Kriegel: "Fast Parallel Similarity Search in Multimedia Databases", *Proceedings of the ACM International Conference on Management of Data (SIGMOD'97)*, pp.1-12, Tucson, AZ, 1997.

[12] S. Berchtold, C. Boehm, D. Keim and H.-P. Kriegel: "A Cost Model for Nearest Neighbor Search in High-Dimensional Data Space", *Proceedings of the 16th ACM SIGACT-SIGMOD-SIGART Symposium on Principles of Database Systems (PODS'97)*, pp.78-86, Tucson, AZ, 1997.

[13] S. Berchtold, D. Keim and H.-P. Kriegel: "The X-tree: an Index Structure for High-Dimensional Data", *Proceedings of the 22nd International Conference on Very Large Databases (VLDB'96)*, pp.28-39, Bombay, India, 1996.

[14] C. Boehm, B. Braunmuller, F. Krebs and H.-P. Kriegel: "Epsilon Grid Order: an Algorithm for the Similarity Join on Massive High-Dimensional Data", *Proceedings of the ACM International Conference on Management of Data (SIGMOD'01)*, Santa Barbara, CA, 2001.

[15] C. Boehm and H.-P. Kriegel: "A Cost Model and Index Architecture for the Similarity Join", *Proceedings of the 17th IEEE International Conference on Data Engineering (ICDE'01)*, pp.411-420, Heidelberg, Germany, 2001.

[16] T. Brinkhoff, H.-P. Kriegel and B. Seeger: "Efficient Processing of Spatial Joins Using R-trees", *Proceedings of the ACM International Conference on Management of Data (SIGMOD'93)*, pp.237-246, Washington, DC, 1993.

[17] T. Brinkhoff, H.-P. Kriegel and B. Seeger: "Parallel Processing of Spatial Joins Using R-trees", *Proceedings of the 12th IEEE International Conference on Data Engineering (ICDE'96)*, pp.258-265, New Orleans, LO, 1996.

[18] S. Ceri and G. Pelagatti: *"Distributed Databases: Principles and Systems"*, McGraw-Hill, 1985.

[19] P.M. Chen, E.K. Lee, G.A. Gibson, R.H. Katz and D.A. Patterson: "RAID, High-Performance, Reliable Secondary Storage", *ACM Computing Surveys*, Vol.26, No.2, pp.145-185, 1994.

[20] S. Chen and D. Towsley: "A Performance Evaluation of RAID Architectures", *IEEE Transactions on Computers*, Vol.45, No.10, pp.1116-1130, 1996.

[21] P. Ciaccia, M. Patella, and P. Zezula: "M-tree: an Efficient Access Method for Similarity Search in Metric Spaces", *Proceedings of the 23rd International Conference on Very Large Databases*, pp.426-435, Athens, Greece, 1997.

[22] A. Corral, Y. Manolopoulos, Y. Theodoridis and M. Vassilakopoulos: "Closest-Pair Queries in Spatial Databases", *Proceedings of the ACM International Conference on Management of Data (SIGMOD'00)*, pp.189-200, Dallas, TX, 2000.

[23] A. Corral, M. Vassilakopoulos and Y. Manolopoulos: "The Impact of Buffering on Closest Pairs Queries Using R-Trees", *Proceedings of the 5th East European Conference on Advances in Databases and Information Systems (ADBIS'01)*, pp.41-54, Vilnius, Lithuania, 2001.

REFERENCES

[24] A. Corral, Y. Manolopoulos, Y. Theodoridis and M. Vassilakopoulos: "Distance Join Queries of Multiple Inputs in Spatial Databases", *Proceedings of the 7th East European Conference on Advances in Databases and Information Systems (ADBIS'03)*, pp.323-338, Dresden, Germany, 2003.

[25] A. Corral, Y. Manolopoulos, Y. Theodoridis and M. Vassilakopoulos: "Algorithms for Processing K-closest-pair Queries in Spatial Databases". *Data and Knowledge Engineering*, Vol.49, No.1, pp.67-104, 2004.

[26] D.J. DeWitt and J. Gray: "Parallel Database Systems - the Future of High Performance Database Systems", *Communications of the ACM*, Vol.35, No.6, pp.85-98, 1992.

[27] R. Fagin: "Combining Fuzzy Information from Multiple Systems", *Proceedings of the 15th ACM SIGACT-SIGMOD-SIGART Symposium on Principles of Database Systems (PODS'96)*, pp.216-226, Montreal, Canada, 1996.

[28] C. Faloutsos: *"Searching Multimedia Databases by Content"*, Kluwer Academic Publishers, 1996.

[29] C. Faloutsos and I. Kamel: "Beyond Uniformity and Independence - Analysis of R-trees Using the Concept of Fractal Dimension", *Proceedings of the 13th ACM SIGACT-SIGMOD-SIGART Symposium on Principles of Database Systems (PODS'94)*, pp.4-13, Minneapolis, MN, 1994.

[30] C. Faloutsos and K.-I. Lin: "Fastmap: a Fast Algorithm for Indexing, Data Mining and Visualization of Traditional and Multimedia Datasets", *Proceedings of the ACM International Conference on Management of Data (SIGMOD'95)*, pp.163-174, Jan Hose, CA, 1995.

[31] C. Faloutsos, M. Ranganathan, and Y. Manolopoulos: "Fast Subsequence Matching in Time-Series Databases", *Proceedings of the ACM International Conference on Management of Data (SIGMOD'94)*, pp.419-429, Minneapolis, MN, 1994.

[32] C. Faloutsos, B. Seeger, A. Traina and C. Traina: "Spatial Join Selectivity Using Power Laws", *Proceedings of the ACM International Conference on Management of Data (SIGMOD'00)*, pp.177-188, Dallas, TX, 2000.

[33] J.H. Friedman, J.L. Bentley and R.A. Finkel: "An Algorithm for Finding the Best Matches in Logarithmic Expected Time", *ACM Transactions on Mathematical Software*, Vol.3, pp.209-226, 1977.

[34] V. Gaede and O. Guenther: "Multidimensional Access Methods", *ACM Computing Surveys*, Vol.30, No.2, pp.170-231, 1998.

[35] R.H. Gueting: "An Introduction to Spatial Database Systems", *The VLDB Journal*, Vol.3, No.4, pp.357-399, 1994.

[36] A. Guttman: "R-trees: a Dynamic Index Structure for Spatial Searching", *Proceedings of the ACM International Conference on Management of Data (SIGMOD'84)*, pp.47-57, Boston, MA, 1984.

[37] M. Hadjieleftheriou, G. Kollios, V.J. Tsotras and D. Gunopoulos: "Efficient Indexing of Spatio-Temporal Objects", *Proceedings of the 8th Conference on Extending Database Technology Conference (EDBT'02)*, pp.251-268, Prague, Czech Republic, 2002.

[38] J. Han, K. Koperski and N. Stefanovic: "GeoMiner: a System Prototype for Spatial Data Mining", *Proceedings of the ACM International Conference on Management of Data (SIGMOD'97)*, pp.553-556, Tucson, AZ, 1997.

[39] T. H. Haveliwala, A. Gionis, D. Klein and P. Indyk: "Evaluating Strategies for Similarity Search on the Web", *Proceedings of 11th World Wide Web Conference (WWW'02)*, Honolulu, Hawaii, 2002.

[40] G. Hjaltason and H. Samet: "Distance Browsing in Spatial Databases", *ACM Transactions on Database Systems*, Vol.24, No.2, pp.265-318, 1999.

[41] E. Hoel and H. Samet: "Performance of Data-Parallel Spatial Operations", *Proceedings of the 20th International Conference on Very Large Databases (VLDB'94)*, pp.156-167, Santiago, Chile, 1994.

[42] Y.-W. Huang, N. Jing and E. Rundesteiner: "Spatial Joins Using R-trees", *Proceedings of the 23rd International Conference on Very Large Data Bases (VLDB'97)*, Athens, Greece, 1997.

[43] Informix Corporation: "The Informix R-tree Index User's Guide", Informix Press, 1999.

[44] Y. Ishikawa, H. Kitagawa and T. Kawashima: "Continual Neighborhood Tracking for Moving Objects Using Adaptive Distances", *Proceedings of the 6th International Database Engineering and Applications Symposium (IDEAS'02)*, pp.54-63, Edmonton, Canada, 2002.

[45] H.V. Jagadish: "Analysis of the Hilbert Curve for Representing Two-Dimensional Space", *Information Processing Letters*, Vol.62, No.1, pp.17-22, 1997.

[46] M. Juergens and H. Lenz: "The Ra*-tree - an Improved R-tree with Materialized Data for Supporting Range Queries on OLAP Data", *Proceedings of the Workshop on Data Warehouse Design and OLAP Technology (DWDOT), 9th International Workshop on Database and Expert Systems Applications (DEXA'98)*, pp.186-191, Vienna, Austria, 1998.

[47] D.V. Kalashnikov, S. Prabhakar, S.E. Hambrusch and W.G. Aref: "Efficient Evaluation of Continuous Range Queries on Moving Objects, *Proceedings of the 13th International Conference on Database and Expert Systems Applications (DEXA'02)*, pp.731-740, Aix-en-Provence, France, 2002.

[48] I. Kamel and C. Faloutsos: "Parallel R-trees", *Proceedings of the ACM International Conference on Management of Data (SIGMOD'92)*, pp.195-204, San Diego, CA, 1992.

[49] I. Kamel and C. Faloutsos: "On Packing R-trees", *Proceedings of the 2nd International Conference on Intelligence and Knowledge Management (CIKM'93)*, pp.490-499, Washington, DC, 1993.

[50] I. Kamel and C. Faloutsos: "Hilbert R-tree - an Improved R-tree Using Fractals", *Proceedings of the 20th International Conference on Very Large Databases (VLDB'94)*, pp.500-509, Santiago, Chile, 1994.

[51] N. Katayama and S. Satoh: "The SR-tree: an Index Structure for High-Dimensional Nearest Neighbor Queries", *Proceedings of the ACM International Conference on Management of Data (SIGMOD'97)*, pp.369-380, Tucson, AZ, 1997.

REFERENCES

[52] D. Knuth: "The Art of Computer Programming: Sorting and Searching", Vol.3, *Addison-Wesley*, 1973.

[53] G. Kollios, D. Gunopoulos and V.J. Tsotras: "Nearest Neighbor Queries in a Mobile Environment", *Proceedings of the International Workshop on Spatio-temporal Database Management*, pp.119-134, Edinburgh, UK, 1999.

[54] G. Kollios, D. Gunopoulos and V.J. Tsotras: "On Indexing Mobile Objects", *Proceedings of the 18th ACM SIGACT-SIGMOD-SIGART Symposium on Principles of Database Systems (PODS'99)*, pp.261-272, Philadelphia, PA, 1999.

[55] K. Koperski and J. Han: "Discovery of Spatial Association Rules in Geographic Information Databases", *Proceedings of the 4th Symposium on Spatial Databases (SSD'95)*, pp.47-66, Portland, ME, 1995.

[56] F. Korn and S. Muthujrishnan: "Influence Sets Based on Reverse Neighbor Queries", *Proceedings of the ACM International Conference on Management of Data (SIGMOD'00)*, pp.201-212, Dallas, TX, 2000.

[57] R.K.V. Kothuri, S. Ravada and D. Abugov: "Quadtree and R-tree Indexes in Oracle Spatial: a Comparison Using GIS Data", *Proceedings of the ACM International Conference on Management of Data (SIGMOD'02)*, pp.546-557, Madison, WI, 2002.

[58] N. Koudas, C. Faloutsos and I. Kamel: "Declustering Spatial Databases on a Multi-computer Architecture", *Proceedings of the 5th Conference on Extending Database Technology Conference (EDBT'96)*, pp.592-614, Avignon, France, 1996.

[59] R. Laurini and D. Thomson: *"Fundamentals of Spatial Information Systems"*, Academic Press, London, 1992.

[60] I. Lazaridis, I. Porkaew and S. Mehrotra: "Dynamic Queries over Mobile Objects", *Proceedings of the 8th Conference on Extending Database Technology Conference (EDBT'02)*, pp.269-286, Prague, Czech Republic, 2002.

[61] S.T. Leutenegger, J.M. Edgington and M.A. Lopez: "STR - a Simple and Efficient Algorithm for R-tree Packing", *Proceedings of the 13th IEEE International Conference on Data Engineering (ICDE'97)*, pp.497-506, Birmingham, UK, 1997.

[62] J. Lieberherr, E.R. Omiecinski and F. Akyildiz: "The Effect of Index Partitioning Schemes on the Performance of Distributed Query Processing", *IEEE Transactions on Knowledge and Data Engineering*, Vol.5, No.3, pp.510-522, 1993.

[63] K. Lin, H.V. Jagadish and C. Faloutsos: "The TV-tree: an Index Structure for High Dimensional Data", *The VLDB Journal*, Vol.3, No.4, pp.517-542, 1995.

[64] M.-L. Lo and C.V. Ravishankar: "Spatial Joins Using Seeded Trees", *Proceedings of the ACM International Conference on Management of Data (SIGMOD'94)*, pp.209-220, Minneapolis, MN, 1994.

[65] M.-L. Lo and C.V. Ravishankar: "Spatial Hash-Joins", *Proceedings of the ACM International Conference on Management of Data (SIGMOD'96)*, pp.247-258, Montreal, Canada, 1996.

[66] D. Lomet and B. Salsberg: "Access Methods for Multiversion Data", *Proceedings of the ACM International Conference on Management of Data (SIGMOD'89)*, pp.315-324, Portland, OR, 1989.

[67] H. Lu, B.-C. Ooi and K.-L. Tan: *"Query Processing in Parallel Relational Database Systems"*, IEEE Computer Society Press, 1994.

[68] G. Lu: *"Multimedia Database Management Systems"*, Artech House, 1999.

[69] N. Mamoulis and D. Papadias: "Slot Index Spatial Join", *IEEE Transactions on Knowledge and Data Engineering*, Vol.15, No.1, 2003.

[70] N. Mamoulis and D. Papadias: "Selectivity Estimation of Complex Spatial Queries", *Proceedings of the 7th International Symposium on Spatial and Temporal Databases (SSTD'01)*, pp.155-174, LA, CA, 2001.

[71] Y. Manolopoulos: "Probability Distributions for Seek Time Evaluation, *Information Sciences*, Vol.60, no.1-2, pp.29-40, 1992.

[72] Y. Manolopoulos, Y. Theodoridis and V. J. Tsotras: *"Advanced Database Indexing"*, Kluwer Academic Publishers, 1999.

[73] Y. Manolopoulos, A. Nanopoulos, A.N. Papadopoulos and Y. Theodoridis: "R-trees Have Grown Everywhere", Technical Report, 2003. Available at http://www.rtreeportal.org/pubs/MNPT03.pdf

[74] Mapinfo WWW site, http://www.mapinfo.com.

[75] C. Mina: "Mapinfo SpatialWare: a Spatial Information Server for RDBMS", *Proceedings of the 24th International Conference on Very Large Databases (VLDB'98)*, pp.704, New York, NY, 1998.

[76] D. Montesi, A. Trombetta and P. A. Dearnley: "A Similarity Based Relational Algebra for Web and Multimedia Data", *Information Processing and Management*, Vol.39, No.2, pp.307-322, 2003.

[77] J. Moreira, C. Ribeiro and T. Abdessalem: "Query Operations for Moving Objects Database Systems", *Proceedings of the 8th ACM Symposium on Advances in Geographic Information Systems (ACM-GIS'00)*, pp.108-114, Washington, DC, 2000.

[78] A. Nanopoulos, Y. Theodoridis and Y. Manolopoulos: "C^2P - Clustering with Closest Pairs", *Proceedings of the 27th International Conference on Very Large Databases (VLDB'01)*, pp.331-340, Roma, Italy, 2001.

[79] A. Nanopoulos, Y. Theodoridis and Y. Manolopoulos: "An Efficient and Effective Algorithm for Density Biased Sampling", *Proceedings of the 11th ACM International Conference on Information and Knowledge Management (CIKM'02)*, pp.398-404, MacLean, VA, 2002.

[80] E. Nardelli and G. Proietti: "Size Estimation of the Intersection Join between Two Line Segment Datasets", *Proceedings ADBIS-DASFAA*, pp.229-238, Prague, Czech Republic, 2000.

[81] M.A. Nascimento and J.R.O. Silva: "Towards Historical R-trees", *Proceedings of the 13th ACM Symposium on Applied Computing (SAC'98)*, pp.235-240, Atlanta, GA, 1998.

REFERENCES

[82] M.A. Nascimento, J.R.O. Silva and Y. Theodoridis: "Evaluation of Access Structures for Discretely Moving Points", *Proceedings of the 1st International Workshop on Spatio-temporal Databases (STDBM'99)*, pp.171-188, Edinburgh, UK, 1999.

[83] W. Niblack, R. Barber, W. Equitz, M. Flickner, E. Glasman, D. Petkovic and P. Yanker: "The QBIC Project: Querying Images by Content Using Color, Texture and Shape", *Proceedings of the SPIE Conference on Storage and Retrieval for Image and Video Databases*, Vol.1908, pp.173-187, San Jose, CA, 1993.

[84] Oracle WWW Site, http://www.oracle.com, http://otn.oracle.com/products/spatial.

[85] J.A. Orenstein: "Spatial Query Processing in an Object Oriented Database System", *Proceedings of the ACM International Conference on Management of Data (SIGMOD'86)*, pp.326-336, Washington, DC, 1986.

[86] T. Ozsu and P. Valduriez: *"Principles of Distributed Database Systems (2nd Edition)"*, Prentice-Hall, 1999.

[87] B.U. Pagel, H.W. Six, H. Toben and P. Widmayer: "Towards an Analysis of Range Query Performance in Spatial Data Structures", *Proceedings of the 12th ACM SIGACT-SIGMOD-SIGART Symposium on Principles of Database Systems (PODS'93)*, pp.214-221, Washington DC, 1993.

[88] D. Papadias, N. Mamoulis and Y. Theodoridis: "Processing and Optimization of Multi-Way Spatial Joins Using R-trees", *Proceedings of the 18th ACM SIGACT-SIGMOD-SIGART Symposium on Principles of Database Systems (PODS'99)*, Philadelphia, PA, 1999.

[89] D. Papadias, P. Kalnis, J. Zhang and Y. Tao: "Efficient OLAP Operations in Spatial Data Warehouses", *Proceedings of the 7th Symposium on Spatio-temporal Databases (SSTD'01)*, pp.443-459, Redondo Beach, CA, 2001.

[90] D. Papadias, Y. Tao, P. Kanlis and J. Zhang: "Indexing Spatio-Temporal Data Warehouses", *Proceedings of the 18th IEEE International Conference on Data Engineering (ICDE'02)*, pp.166-175, San Jose, CA, 2002.

[91] D. Papadias, J. Zhang, N. Mamoulis and Y. Tao: "Query Processing in Spatial Network Databases", *Proceedings of the 29th International Conference on Very Large Data Bases (VLDB'03)*, pp.802-813, Berlin, Germany, 2003.

[92] A.N. Papadopoulos and Y. Manolopoulos: "Parallel Processing of Nearest Neighbor Queries in Declustered Spatial Data", *Proceedings of the 4th ACM Workshop on Advances on Geographic Information Systems (ACM-GIS'96)*, pp.37-43, Rockville, MD, 1996.

[93] A.N. Papadopoulos and Y. Manolopoulos: "Performance of Nearest Neighbor Queries in R-trees", *Proceedings of the 4th International Conference on Database Theory (ICDT'97)*, pp.394-408, Delphi, Greece, 1997.

[94] A.N. Papadopoulos, Y. Manolopoulos: "Nearest Neighbor Queries in Shared-Nothing Environments", *Geoinformatica*, Vol.1, No.4, pp.369-392, 1997.

[95] A.N. Papadopoulos, Y. Manolopoulos: "Similarity Query Processing using Disk Arrays", *Proceedings of the ACM International Conference on Management of Data (SIGMOD'98)*, pp.225-236, Seattle, WA, 1998.

[96] A.N. Papadopoulos, Y. Manolopoulos: "Distributed Processing of Similarity Queries", *Distributed and Parallel Databases*, Vol.9, No.1, pp.67-92, 2001.

[97] A.N. Papadopoulos, P. Rigaux, M. Scholl: "A Performance Evaluation of Spatial Join Processing Strategies", *Proceedings of the 6th International Symposium on Spatial Databases (SSD'99)*, pp.286-307, Hong-Kong, China, 1999.

[98] J. Paredaens: "Spatial Databases, the Final Frontier", *Proceedings of the 5th International Conference on Database Theory (ICDT'95)*, pp.14-32, Prague, Czech Republic, 1995.

[99] D.A. Patterson, G. Gibson and R.H. Katz: "A Case for Redundant Arrays of Inexpensive Disks (RAID)", *Proceedings of the ACM International Conference on Management of Data (SIGMOD'88)*, pp.109-116, Chicago, IL, 1988.

[100] D. Pfoser, C.S. Jensen and Y. Theodoridis: "Novel Approaches to the Indexing of Moving Object Trajectories", *Proceedings of the 26th International Conference on Very Large Databases (VLDB'00)*, pp.395-406, 2000.

[101] F.P. Preparata and M. I. Samos: *"Computational Geometry"*, Springer-Verlag, 1985.

[102] G. Proietti and C. Faloutsos: "Analysis of Range Queries and Self-Spatial Join Queries on Real Region Datasets Stored using an R-tree", *IEEE Transactions on Knowledge and Data Engineering*, Vol.12, No.5, pp.751-762, 2000.

[103] K. Raptopoulou, A. N. Papadopoulos and Y. Manolopoulos: "Fast Nearest Neighbor Query Processing in Moving-Object Databases", *Geoinformatica*, Vol.7, No.2, pp.113-137, 2003.

[104] P. Rigaux, M. Scholl and A. Voisard: *"Spatial Databases with Applications to GIS"*, Morgan Kaufmann, 2002.

[105] M. T. Roth, M. Arya, L. M. Haas, M. J. Carey, W. F. Cody, R. Fagin, P. M. Schwarz, J. Thomas II and E. L. Wimmers: "The Garlic Project", *Proceedings of the ACM International Conference on Management of Data (SIGMOD'96)*, Montreal, Canada, 1996.

[106] N. Roussopoulos, S. Kelley and F. Vincent: "Nearest Neighbor Queries", *Proceedings of the ACM International Conference on Management of Data (SIGMOD'95)*, pp.71-79, San Jose, CA, 1995.

[107] N. Roussopoulos and D. Leifker: "Direct Spatial Search on Pictorial Databases Using Packed R-trees", *Proceedings of the ACM International Conference on Management of Data (SIGMOD'85)*, pp.17-31, Austin, TX, 1985.

[108] C. Ruemmler and J. Wilkes: "An Introduction to Disk Drive Modeling", *IEEE Computer*, Vol.27, No.3, pp.17-28, 1994.

[109] Y. Sakurai, M. Yoshikawa, A. Uemura and H. Kojima: "The A-tree: an Index Structure for High-Dimensional Spaces Using Relative Approximation", *Proceedings of the 26th International Conference on Very Large Databases (VLDB'00)*, pp.516-526, Cairo, Egypt, 2000.

REFERENCES

[110] S. Saltenis, C.S. Jensen, S. Leutenegger and M. Lopez: "Indexing the Positions of Continuously Moving Objects", *Proceedings of the ACM International Conference on Management of Data (SIGMOD'00)*, pp.331-342, Santa Barbara, CA, 2000.

[111] H. Samet: *"The Design and Analysis of Spatial Data Structures"*, Addison-Wesley, Reading MA, 1990.

[112] H. Samet: *"Applications of Spatial Data Structures"*, Addison-Wesley, Reading MA, 1990.

[113] B. Seeger and P.A. Larson: "Multi-Disk B-trees", *Proceedings of the ACM International Conference on Management of Data (SIGMOD'91)*, pp.436-445, Denver, CO, 1991.

[114] T. Seidl and H.-P. Kriegel: "Optimal Multi-Step k-Nearest Neighbor Search", *Proceedings of the ACM International Conference on Management of Data (SIGMOD'88)*, pp.154-165, Seattle, WA, 1998.

[115] T. Sellis, N. Roussopoulos and C. Faloutsos: "The R^+-tree - a Dynamic Index for Multidimensional Objects", *Proceedings of the 13th International Conference on Very Large Databases (VLDB'87)*, pp.507-518, Brighton, UK, 1987.

[116] J. C. Shafer and R. Agrawal: "Parallel Algorithms for High-dimensional Proximity Joins for Data Mining Applications", *Proceedings of the 23rd International Conference on Very Large Data Bases (VLDB'97)*, pp.176-185, Athens, Greece, 1997.

[117] C. Shahabi, M.R. Kolahdouzan and M. Sharifzadeh: "A Road Network Embedding Technique for K-Nearest Neighbor Search in Moving Object Databases", *Proceedings of the 10th ACM Workshop on Advances on Geographic Information Systems (ACM-GIS'02)*, McLean, VA, 2002.

[118] S. Shekhar, S. Ravada, V. Kumar, D. Chubb and G. Turner: "Declustering and Load-Balancing Methods for Parallelizing Geographical Information Systems", *IEEE Transactions on Knowledge and Data Engineering*, Vol.10, No.4, pp.632-655, 1998.

[119] S. Shekhar and S. Chawla: *"Spatial Databases: A Tour"*, Prentice Hall, 2003.

[120] S. Shekhar and J.S. Yoo: "Processing In-Route Nearest Neighbor Queries: a Comparison of Alternative Approaches", *Proceedings of the 11th ACM Workshop on Advances on Geographic Information Systems (ACM-GIS'03)*, New Orleans, LO, 2003.

[121] K. Shim, R. Srikant and R. Agrawal: "High-Dimensional Similarity Joins", *Proceedings of the 13th IEEE International Conference on Data Engineering (ICDE'97)*, Birmingham, UK, 1997.

[122] A.P. Sistla, O. Wolfson, S. Chamberlain and S. Dao: "Modeling and Querying Moving Objects", *Proceedings of the 13th IEEE International Conference on Data Engineering (ICDE'97)*, pp.422-432, Birmingham, UK, 1997.

[123] Z. Song and N. Roussopoulos: "K-NN Search for Moving Query Point", *Proceedings of the 7th Symposium on Spatio-temporal Databases (SSTD'01)*, pp.79-96, Redondo Beach, CA, 2001.

[124] Z. Song and N. Roussopoulos: "Hashing Moving Objects", *Proceedings of the 2nd International Conference on Mobile Data Management (MDM'01)*, pp.161-172, Hong Kong, China, 2001.

[125] I. Stanoi, D. Agrawal and A. Abbadi: "Reverse Nearest Neighbor Queries for Dynamic Datasets", *Proceedings of the 5th Workshop on Research Issues in Data Mining and Knowledge Discovery (DMKD'00)*, pp.44-53, Dallas, TX, 2000.

[126] W.R. Stevens: *"UNIX Network Programming"*, Prentice-Hall, 1990.

[127] M. Stonebraker, T. Sellis and E. Hanson: "An Analysis of Rule Indexing Implementations in Data Base Systems", *Proceedings of the 1st Conference on Expert Database Systems*, pp.465-476, Charleston, SC, 1986.

[128] M. Stonebraker, J. Frew, K. Gardels and J. Meredith: "The Sequoia 2000 Storage Benchmark", *Proceedings of the ACM International Conference on Management of Data (SIGMOD'93)*, pp.2-11, Washington, DC, 1993.

[129] Y. Tao and D. Papadias: "MV3R-tree - a Spatio-Temporal Access Method for Timestamp and Interval Queries", *Proceedings of the 27th International Conference on Very Large Databases (VLDB'01)*, pp.431-440, 2001.

[130] Y. Tao and D. Papadias: "Time-Parameterized Queries in Spatio-Temporal Databases" *Proceedings of the ACM International Conference on Management of Data (SIGMOD'02)*, pp.334-345, Madison, WI, 2002.

[131] Y. Tao, D. Papadias and Q. Shen: "Continuous Nearest Neighbor Search", *Proceedings of the 28th International Conference on Very Large Databases (VLDB'02)*, pp.287-298, 2002.

[132] Y. Tao, D. Papadias and J. Zhang: "Aggregate Processing of Planar Points", *Proceedings of the 8th Conference on Extending Database Technology Conference (EDBT'02)*, pp.682-700, Prague, Czech Republic, 2002.

[133] Y. Tao, J. Zhang, D. Papadias and N. Mamoulis: " An Efficient Cost Model for Optimization of Nearest Neighbor Search in Low and Medium Dimensional Spaces", *IEEE Transactions on Knowledge and Data Engineering*, 2004.

[134] Y. Tao, D. Papadias and X. Lian: "Reverse kNN Search in Arbitrary Dimensionality", *Proceedings of the 30th International Conference on Very Large Databases (VLDB'04)*, Toronto, Canada, 2004.

[135] Y. Theodoridis and T. Sellis: "A Model for the Prediction of R-tree Performance", *Proceedings of the 15th ACM SIGACT-SIGMOD-SIGART Symposium on Principles of Database Systems (PODS'96)*, pp.161-171, Montreal, Canada, 1996.

[136] Y. Theodoridis, T. Sellis, A.N. Papadopoulos and Y. Manolopoulos: "Specifications for Efficient Indexing in Spatiotemporal Databases", *Proceedings of the 10th IEEE Conference in Scientific and Statistical Databases (SSDBM'98)*, pp.123-132, Capri, Italy, 1998.

[137] Y. Theodoridis, M. Vazirgiannis and T. Sellis: "Spatio-temporal Indexing for Large Multimedia Applications", *Proceedings of the 3rd IEEE International Conference on Multimedia Computing and Systems (ICMCS'96)*, pp.441-448, Hiroshima, Japan, 1996.

[138] TIGER/Line Files, 1994 Technical Documentation / prepared by the Bureau of the Census, Washington, DC, 1994.

REFERENCES

[139] C. Traina, A. Traina, B. Seeger and C. Faloutsos: "Slim-trees: High Performance Metric Trees Minimizing Overlap Between Nodes", *Proceedings of the 7th International Conference on Extending Database Technology (EDBT'00)*, pp.51-65, Konstanz, Germany, 2000.

[140] C. Traina, A. Traina, B. Seeger and C. Faloutsos: "Fast Indexing and Visualization of Metric Data Sets using Slim-Trees", *IEEE Transactions on Knowledge and Data Engineering*, Vol.14, No.2, pp.244-260, 2002.

[141] P. Trianafillou and C. Faloutsos: " Overlay Striping and Optimal Parallel I/O for Modern Applications", *Parallel Computing*, Vol.24, No.1, pp.21-43, 1998.

[142] D. White and R. Jain: "Similarity Indexing with the SS-tree", *Proceedings of the 12th IEEE International Conference on Data Engineering (ICDE'96)*, pp.516-523, New Orleans, LO, 1996.

[143] R. Williams et al.: "R^*: an Overview of the Architecture", *IBM Research Report*, San Jose, Calif., RJ3325, 1981.

[144] O. Wolfson, B. Xu and S. Chamberlain: "Location Prediction and Queries for Tracking Moving Objects", *Proceedings of the 16th IEEE International Conference on Data Engineering (ICDE'00)*, pp.687-688, San Diego, CA, 2000.

[145] O. Wolfson, B. Xu, S. Chamberlain and L. Jiang: "Moving Objects Databases: Issues and Solutions", *Proceedings of the 10th IEEE Conference in Scientific and Statistical Databases (SSDBM'98)*, pp.111-122, Capri, Italy, 1998.

[146] X. Xu, J. Han and W. Lu: "RT-tree: an Improved R-tree Index Structure for Spatio-Temporal Databases", *Proceedings of the Symposium on Spatial Data Handling (SDH'90)*, pp.1040-1049, 1990.

[147] P. Zezula, P. Savino, F. Rabitti, G. Amato, P. Ciaccia: "Processing M-trees with Parallel Resources", *Proceedings of the 8th International Workshop on Research Issues in Data Engineering (RIDE'98)*, pp.147-154, 1998.

[148] B. Zheng and D. Lee: "Semantic Caching in Location-Dependent Query Processing", *Proceedings of the 7th Symposium on Spatio-temporal Databases (SSTD'01)*, pp.97-116, Redondo Beach, CA, 2001.

[149] Y. Zhou, S. Shekhar and M. Coyle: "Disk Allocation Methods for Parallelizing Grid Files", *Proceedings of the 10th IEEE International Conference on Data Engineering (ICDE'94)*, pp.243-252, Houston, TX, 1994.

Index

A-tree, 20

B^+-tree, 13, 16, 77

candidate set, 7, 153
continuous queries, 50

data mining, 19, 153
data warehouse, 19, 128
DFT, 9, 32
dimensionality curse, 9, 20
disk array, 76, 87, 98, 107
disk characteristics, 100
distributed database system, 75
distribution transparency, 76

edit distance, 28
ethernet, 118, 146
Euclidean distance, 5, 25, 26, 32, 38, 41, 54, 60, 128, 153

false alarms, 7, 27
false dismissals, 32, 117
FastMap, 28
FCFS, 99
filter-refinement, 7, 32, 153
fractal dimension, 38, 45
    correlation, 41
    Hausdorff, 42
fragmentation, 83
    horizontal, 83
    vertical, 83

GEMINI, 8

Hilbert packed R-tree, 18, 44, 117
Hilbert R-tree, 16, 125

IBM DB2, 10
IBM Informix, 10

incremental, 35, 99
independent R-trees, 77

k-d-tree, 29

L_p norm, 26

M-tree, 28, 108
Manhattan distance, 25
Mapinfo SpatialWare, 10
MAXDIST, 65, 89, 113, 145
metric space, 28
MINDIST, 29, 38, 45, 63, 88, 105, 113, 144, 150
minimum bounding rectangle (MBR), 7
MINMAXDIST, 29, 39, 88, 113
multimedia applications, 31
multiplexed R-tree, 79

network of workstations, 76, 82, 109, 127, 142

object approximation, 7
Oracle, 10

packed R-tree, 18
parallel architecture, 76, 127
parallel architectures, 81
parallel database system, 75, 109
parallel performance measures, 80
parallelism
    CPU, 76
    I/O, 76
Poisson distribution, 100
proximity index, 80
pruning rules, 30, 54, 65, 88, 106, 150

query execution plan, 5, 37, 154

R*-tree, 16
R+-tree, 15

R-tree, 8, 13, 77
    dynamic variants, 15
    static variants, 17
R-tree characteristics, 14
RAID, 76
ranking, 35
regression, 111, 125
round-robin, 77, 80, 82, 110

seeds, 14
sequential scanning, 6, 102
Sequoia 2000, 98, 118
Slim-tree, 28
space-filling curves, 16, 82, 110
spatial data types, 3
    line segment, 3, 53
    point, 3
    polygon, 4
    rectangle, 4
spatial database, xvii, 3, 11, 154

spatial queries, 4
    closest-pairs, 5
    directional, 4
    distance, 4
    join, 5
    nearest neighbors, 5
    range query, 5
    topological, 4
split points, 52
split policies, 14
STR packed R-tree, 18
super nodes, 78

TIGER, 19, 98, 118
time-parameterized queries, 51
TPR-tree, 19, 50, 62
TV-tree, 9, 20

X-tree, 9, 20